Blender Baby Food
Second Edition

Over 175 Recipes
for Healthy Homemade Meals

Nicole Young
Nadine Day, RD, Nutritional Adviser

For complete cataloguing information, see page 210.

Disclaimer
The recipes in this book have been carefully tested by our kitchen and our tasters. To the best of our knowledge, they are safe and nutritious for ordinary use and users. For those people with food or other allergies, or who have special food requirements or health issues, please read the suggested contents of each recipe carefully and determine whether or not they may create a problem for you. All recipes are used at the risk of the consumer.

We cannot be responsible for any hazards, loss or damage that may occur as a result of any recipe use.

For those with special needs, allergies, requirements or health problems, in the event of any doubt, please contact your medical adviser prior to the use of any recipe.

Design & Production: PageWave Graphics Inc.
Editor: Sue Sumeraj
Food Tester: Jennifer MacKenzie
Proofreader: Sheila Wawanash
Index: Belle Wong
Front Cover Photography: ©iStockphoto.com/Paul Roux
Interior Photography: Tango

We acknowledge the financial support of the Government of Canada through the Book Publishing Industry Development Program (BPIDP) for our publishing activities.

Published by Robert Rose Inc.
120 Eglinton Avenue East, Suite 800, Toronto, Ontario, Canada M4P 1E2
Tel: (416) 322-6552   Fax: (416) 322-6936
www.robertrose.ca

Printed in Canada

1 2 3 4 5 6 7 8 9 TCP 19 18 17 16 15 14 13 12 11

Mixed Sources
Product group from well-managed forests and other controlled sources
www.fsc.org Cert no. SW-COC-000952
© 1996 Forest Stewardship Council
FSC

Contents

Preface

A month before I gave birth to my first child, I attended a birthday party for a friend's son. I observed the "veteran" parents escorting their toddlers to the table at mealtime and stared in utter amazement at my friend's son, who sat proudly in his high chair and proceeded to eat his first birthday meal of blanched broccoli and green beans, strips of red peppers and carrots, while the neighboring children pushed away everything but fish crackers. What had my friend done to produce this veggie- and hummus-loving pita eater? As I watched him eat his body weight in produce, I heard his mother's words: "I made all his food from scratch." I was sold.

Over the past five years, I have taught hundreds of classes to parents and caregivers about the merits of preparing their own food for babies. We discuss the issues of variety, quality, ability to graduate textures and cost-effectiveness. I demonstrate the simplicity of preparing a variety of purées, even for sleep-deprived parents whose last wish is to have an extra task added to their baby-dominated lives. All of these details are included in Nadine's comprehensive introduction.

While it has been many years since I had to make my own purées, the benefits are undeniable. I have two healthy eaters who still enjoy treats but don't turn their noses up at a platter of fresh veggies. I am fortunate.

More than anything, I want this book to inspire you to give making your own baby food a try. May you and your child have many happy memories of the food from these pages...

Acknowledgments

I have to thank Liam and Claire for being my inspiration to make baby food and David for giving me our inspirations and providing the time, support and encouragement to finish this book. I love you all more than food! It was the ideal year for taste testers, because we had 11 babies born to friends, and I am very appreciative of all the discerning palates. May you all be healthy eaters with massive appetites!

Thanks to Andrew Chase for recommending me, publisher Bob Dees for giving me the project, and my lawyer, sister and friend Danielle for looking out for me since we were little. Thanks also to my sister Stephanie for her blender wisdom. I'd like to express my gratitude to Nadine Day, registered dietitian extraordinaire, for her advice and nutritional analysis, and to Judy Coveney for introducing us. Thanks to Sue Sumeraj, our patient editor, for teaching me the process and making me seem literate.

Finally, eternal thanks to my mom and dad for showing me what it means to be a great parent and teaching me that anything is possible.

— Nicole Young

I would like to thank my daughter, Grace, for teaching me more about infant feeding than any course I have ever taken. Thanks also to my husband, Simon, and my mom for all their support and for making sure I have a quiet space in which to write. And to my dad, whose voice always echoes that I can do whatever I set my mind to. I love you all so much.

I am in debt to Nicole Young and Judy Coveney for encouraging me to take on this project. Convincing me was a challenge, because they contacted me on my first day of being a new mom.

Special thanks to my friends and colleagues Liane Evans and Karem Kalin for critiquing the facts and to our editor, Sue Sumeraj, for making my words sound great.

This has been a very valuable and rewarding experience, and I am so happy I took advantage of the opportunity.

— Nadine Day

Introduction

It is exciting when your baby starts to eat solid food. He is making an important step towards toddlerhood! Helping a child progress through this stage can be very rewarding. Parents often have many questions about when to start solids and what to feed when. The good news is that it is not an exact science. There are a few suggested guidelines, but the real judge is your baby. He will give you cues that he is ready to move on to a new flavor or texture.

Making your own baby food may seem challenging at first, but it doesn't have to be. *Blender Baby Food* provides many recipes and tips that will make baby food fun and exciting for you and your baby. Whether you choose to make all of your own baby food or just some of it, the blender is a great way to offer new flavors in a baby-friendly texture. Even when your child is eating table food, there is always room for a fruit smoothie or a nutritious dip.

This latest version of the book contains:

- 25 exciting new recipes;
- updated guidelines on starting solids, consistent with updates from leading pediatric associations;
- updated menu plans, including one for babies who have been mostly breastfed;
- lots of additional tips and tricks for making your own baby food; and
- 16 brand new and delectable color photographs.

When to Start Solids

The American Academy of Pediatrics and Health Canada recommend starting complementary foods at six months. Complementary foods means foods *in addition* to breast milk or formula. At this point, babies are both mentally and physiologically ready to accept solid foods. But every baby is different when it comes to readiness to start solid foods. Your baby may be ready if she:

- can sit alone or with minimal support;
- opens her mouth when she sees something coming towards her face or mouth;

- turns her head away when she does not want it;
- closes her lips over the spoon; and
- seems interested in what you are eating.

Follow your baby's lead. It may take one or two months before she is eating a few tablespoons of solid food at one time. Infants can thrive on breast milk or formula alone until six months, so there is no need to rush into solid foods.

What Foods to Start When

Children progress at very different rates. Let your child help you assess when he is ready to start making the move from exclusively breast or bottle feedings to table foods.

At **six months** of age, iron stores your baby acquired from you during pregnancy start to decline, and an additional source of iron is required. This is particularly true for babies who are mostly breastfed because breast milk is low in iron. Most infant formulas have been fortified with the mineral.

Iron-fortified infant cereal is usually the first solid food introduced to infants. It is great as a first food because you can control the consistency of the cereal, which makes it easier for your child to learn to swallow properly. It is best to start with single-grain cereals, such as rice or barley, introduced one at a time to help your child's body adapt to the new food and so you can watch for symptoms of an allergic reaction. Then you can phase in oatmeal and finally mixed-grain cereals containing wheat.

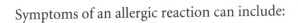

Symptoms of an allergic reaction can include:

- anaphylaxis (a life-threatening reaction);
- stomach pain;
- stomach cramps;
- diarrhea;
- rash around the mouth or anus;
- nausea;
- vomiting;
- itching (throat, mouth, eyes);
- hives;
- swelling;
- stuffy or runny nose;
- shortness of breath; and
- difficulty swallowing.

The severity of the reaction depends on the severity of the allergy. If you suspect that your child is having an allergic reaction to foods, see your doctor.

Once your child is eating 2 to 3 tablespoons (30 to 45 mL) of single-grain cereal a couple of times a day, you can start to introduce puréed meats, puréed dried beans and lentils, vegetables and fruits. It does not matter whether you start with vegetables or with fruits. Some people find that their children eat more vegetables if they were offered before fruit. Some don't find any difference. There is no evidence that starting vegetables before fruit will increase your child's love of vegetables later in life. Let your child take the lead, but don't give up if he rejects a food on the first attempt. He might just be surprised by the new flavor.

Meat and beans are good sources of iron and can be used as an early food, especially for babies who have been mostly breastfed. Some children have initial difficulties accepting meat products. Make sure the meats are puréed or finely minced with a little water or broth or with a vegetable. There are many creative meat and vegetable combinations in this book. Puréed foods should have the consistency of smooth pudding, while the texture of minced food will be similar to rice pudding. The longer you run your blender, the smoother the consistency will be. Puréed foods are best for first foods. Once your child is accepting the purée, you can move to minced foods and then to those that have been finely diced.

It will be much easier for you to identify potential allergies or intolerances if you introduce new foods five to seven days apart. This is especially important if you have a family history of food allergies.

Continue breastfeeding or formula feeding on demand while you are introducing solids. Breast milk or formula is your child's best source of protein, fat and many vitamins and minerals, such as calcium. At this point, solid foods should be *in addition* to your regular breast milk or formula feedings.

At **eight months**, your child will probably be eating a variety of meats, beans, vegetables and fruits, as well as iron-fortified infant cereals, two to three times a day. He can now begin to try other grain products, such as strips of bread, toast, crackers and wheat cereals. Make sure these foods are cut or broken into bite-size pieces.

At this age, your baby will also be ready to try fish, egg yolks and tofu. (Egg whites have been shown to cause an allergic reaction in some children; therefore, it is recommended that you wait until your child is at least one year old before you introduce them.) To be on the safe side, introduce new foods five to seven days apart. Let your baby get comfortable with a new flavor before you introduce the next one.

At this age, babies are ready to try using a cup. Breast milk, formula and water are good choices to offer in a regular cup or a "sippy" cup. Juice is not necessary, especially if your child is eating vegetables and fruits. It is good practice for children to learn to eat rather than drink their fruit. Whole fruits have the added benefit of fiber, which is important to good health. When given the choice, many toddlers will drink their calories, and the juice cup can sometimes be abused. Juice is also high in sugar and may lead to increased dental cavities. If you serve juice, make sure it is 100% fruit juice diluted with water, and serve no more than 4 ounces (125 mL) per day.

At **nine to twelve months**, your child can start to eat dairy foods such as yogurt and cheese. At this time, he can usually eat adapted table food: diced cooked vegetables and fruits, tender chopped meats and casseroles with noodles cut up.

It is important to introduce your child to a variety of textures, as this helps him learn to chew and swallow properly and safely. The following chart gives an idea of what textures are appropriate at what age:

TIP: Use the large side of a grater to cut up harder fruits and vegetables such as carrots, apples and pears. Finely dice softer cooked foods into $1/2$-inch (1 cm) cubes (the size of the tip of your pinky finger).

6 months	Very watery purées, the consistency of watered-down pudding
7 months	Slightly lumpy minced foods, the consistency of rice or tapioca pudding
8 to 12 months	Soft foods, diced or shredded
12 months and over	Adapted family foods (soft foods or harder foods diced into bite-size pieces)

At this age, your child's main beverage is still breast milk or formula. Whole pasteurized cow's milk can be started after one year and can replace formula or be given in addition to breast milk. It is not appropriate for children to be on a fat-restricted diet; they need the extra energy and essential fatty acids that full-fat (3.5% M.F.) milk provides for proper growth and development. At two years, toddlers can be switched to 2% or 1% milk.

Age Appropriateness

The recipes in this book are broken into chapters according to the age at which foods generally become appropriate and tolerable to most babies. Here's a general idea of what foods are appropriate when:

6 months	Meats, beans, lentils, single vegetables and fruits (after single-grain cereal has been introduced); mixed meats, beans, vegetables and fruits (after all ingredients in the recipe have been introduced separately)
8 months	Pasta, rice, other grains, fish, egg yolks, tofu
9 months	Yogurt, cheese
12 months	Full-fat (3.5% M.F.) milk, honey, egg whites. Talk to your doctor about adding nuts and nut butters.

Remember, these are just suggestions. Your pediatrician or family doctor may suggest otherwise, especially if your family has a history of allergies or intolerances.

Again, when it comes to textures and flavors, let your baby guide you: she will let you know when she is ready for something new.

Meal Plans

At the beginning of each chapter, you will find meal plans to help you get started. Each recipe makes about 4 to 8 servings. To save time and freezer space, use the same meal plan four days in a row, then move on to a new meal plan. Infants and toddlers do not crave variety the way adults do.

Remember, children are all different sizes and have different needs. Infants and toddlers have erratic eating patterns and may eat more one day and less the next. Over time it will equal out.

Safety Concerns

Honey

The American Academy of Pediatrics and Health Canada recommend that honey not be fed to children who are less than one year old. Honey is a risk factor for infant botulism. Botulism is life-threatening food poisoning caused by the presence of the botulinus toxin produced by the *Clostridium botulinum* bacterium. The amount of botulism present in honey should not be harmful to adults, but it is harmful to infants. Make sure to read packages and recipes carefully, as honey is often used to sweeten foods.

TIP: For recipes with a combination of ingredients, it is best to first introduce each food separately so you can watch for any food reactions.

Eggs

Eggshells occasionally become contaminated with salmonella bacteria. Cook all eggs very well and avoid all foods containing raw eggs.

Choking

Here are some guidelines to help you avoid this hazard:

- Supervise your infant at all times while he is eating.
- Make sure mealtimes are quiet and calm.
- Don't make your child laugh while he is eating: it could cause him to inhale food.
- Avoid hard, small, round and sticky foods, which can block the airway (see the examples in the chart below for making such foods safe).
- Don't give the following foods to children under four: popcorn, hard candies, gum, cough drops, raisins, peanuts or other nuts, sunflower seeds, fish with bones, or foods with toothpicks or skewers.

Preparing Foods Safely

Food	Unsafe preparation	Safer preparation
Hot dogs/wieners	Sliced into rounds	Cut lengthwise and then into half-moons
Raw carrots or hard fresh fruits	Whole or large pieces	Grated
Fruits with pits	Whole	Diced with pits removed
Grapes	Whole	Chopped
Peanut butter	Spoonful or alone	Spread thinly on crackers or bread

Bottles

Babies should be supervised while using a bottle. The safest way to feed a bottle is when your child is sitting upright in a quiet setting where he is not distracted from eating. The bottle should not be given "propped up" by a blanket or towel or when your child is lying down, walking, running or in a car.

Food Allergies

Food allergies occur when the body has an adverse response to an ingested food. The symptoms may include anaphylaxis (a life-threatening reaction), stomach pain, diarrhea, rash around the mouth or anus, nausea, vomiting, stomach cramps, itching (throat, mouth, eyes), hives, swelling, stuffy nose, runny nose, shortness of breath and difficulty swallowing. The severity of the reaction depends on the severity of the allergy. If you suspect that your child is having an adverse reaction, see your doctor.

The development of a food allergy is mostly genetic: if a child's mother, father or sibling is allergic to a food, she has an increased chance of also being allergic to that food. But food allergies can also develop when a potentially allergenic food is introduced to an infant too early. The chance of developing an allergy is higher in the first year of life because the infant's intestinal system is more permeable to (allows in) food allergens. Milk, eggs, peanuts, soy, nuts and wheat are responsible for 95% of all food allergies. Studies indicate that 2% to 8% of infants and children under three will experience food hypersensitivity. However, many children outgrow their allergies by their fifth birthday. If your family has a history of food allergies, or if you have any concerns, talk to your doctor before introducing any potentially allergenic food.

If your child is diagnosed with a food allergy or intolerance, talk to your doctor or dietitian about any nutritional deficiencies that may result. For example, if your child is allergic to or cannot tolerate milk, she may have to take a calcium supplement or increase her consumption of other calcium-rich foods to meet her needs.

Making Your Own Baby Food

Baby food doesn't have to come in jars. Making your own at home is not difficult. Baby food is simply strained, puréed or mashed adult food, just a different version of the food you prepare for yourself. Here are four good reasons to make your own baby food:

- You know what's in it.
- You can tailor the texture to your baby's preferences.
- You can shape your baby's tastes and help him learn what fresh foods taste like.
- You can help him learn the taste of foods common to your family or culture.

Tips for Making Baby Food

- Work under the most sanitary conditions possible:
  - Scrub your hands with hot water and soap, rinse and dry with a clean towel before fixing your baby's food, before feeding your baby and after changing your baby's diapers.
  - Scrub all working surfaces with soap and hot water.
  - Scrub all equipment with soap and hot water, and rinse well.
- Prepare fresh fruits and vegetables by scrubbing, paring or peeling and removing seeds.
- Prepare meats by removing all bones, skin, connective tissue, gristle and fat.
- Cook foods, when necessary, by boiling them until tender in a small covered saucepan with a small amount of water. The amount of water is important: the less water used, the more nutrients stay in the food.
- Purée food using a blender, food processor, baby food grinder, spoon or fork. Grind up tough foods. Cut food into small pieces or thin slices. Remove seeds and pits from fruit.
- There's no need to add salt or sugar. Try a bit of lemon juice as both a preservative and a natural flavor enhancer.
- Avoid deep-frying, which adds unhealthy fats to foods.
- Don't feel you have to prepare separate meals for your baby. You can simply take portions of your adult food (before you add strong seasonings) and grind or mash it to a consistency appropriate for your baby.
- Make enough purée for several meals and store as directed on the next page or in the recipe.

To Store

- If you're not using puréed food right away, refrigerate or freeze it in portioned containers. Most refrigerated foods will last up to three days (exceptions are noted in the recipes).
- To freeze: Pour cooled, puréed food into paper cupcake liners or a clean ice cube tray and cover with plastic wrap or foil. When frozen solid (after about twenty-four hours), transfer cubes to a resealable freezer bag labeled with the contents and date.
- Rotate stock as the supermarket does, putting the most recently frozen foods behind the previously frozen ones. Homemade baby foods can be safely kept frozen for three months.

To Thaw/Reheat

- For slow thawing, place a day's worth of baby food in a sealed container in the refrigerator. It will thaw in about four hours. Do not thaw at room temperature, as bacteria could grow in the food while it is thawing.
- For fast thawing and heating, heat frozen cubes in a heat-resistant container in a pan of hot water over low heat or in the microwave.
- Stir the food well and test it with a finger to be sure it's not too hot (especially if you use a microwave). Babies generally like their food close to room temperature.
- Discard any food that has been heated and not eaten.

Equipment Needed

- **Blender:** All of the recipes in this book work best using the blender.
- **Fine-mesh sieve or strainer:** Use for juices, soft fruits and vegetables (but not meats). Press food through the sieve with the back of a spoon — to remove seeds, for example.
- **Spoons, forks and a potato masher:** Use to mash soft foods — most canned fruits, egg yolks, bananas and potatoes — to the right consistency.
- **Food mill:** The smaller-size baby food mill is similar to the larger version and can be purchased in the baby section of department stores. It can be used at home or when traveling. It is great for puréeing soft vegetables, fruits, pasta and rice.

- **Plastic ice cube trays:** Use to freeze extra food as explained opposite.

Additional Useful Equipment

- Food processor
- Hand-held blender
- Vegetable brush and peeler
- Saucepan with lid
- Vegetable steamer
- Egg poacher
- Roasting pan
- Cookie sheet
- Muffin tin
- Ovenproof glass cups
- Measuring cups and spoons
- Ladle
- Spatula
- Sharp paring knife
- Cutting board
- Grater
- Storage jars (4 oz/125 mL)
- Small freezer bags
- Waxed paper
- Freezer tape
- Marking pen

Twelve to Twenty-four Months: Learning Healthy Eating

At one year old, your baby officially becomes a toddler. She is on the move, and it may seem like she has no desire to eat regular meals and snacks. This is normal. Try to give your toddler frequent small feedings rather than the traditional meals and snacks. Providing toddlers with healthy food choices gives them the energy and nutrients they need to grow and helps them develop a taste for a wide variety of foods. You will have more success if you feed your toddler nutritious foods when she is hungry than you will if you force her to sit and eat at certain times. This does not mean that toddlers should not be a part of family meals. Your toddler learns a lot from sitting at the family table and seeing how the rest of the family enjoys healthy meals together.

After their first year, children's growth rates slow down. That is why toddlers' eating habits may seem minimal, erratic and unpredictable. During the first year of life, children typically triple their birth weight, and their length increases by 50%. However, their weight will not quadruple until age two, and their length will not double again until age four. They simply do not need the volume of food they did in the first year. Letting your child tell you when she is hungry allows her to follow her own instincts when it comes to regulating food intake. Your job as a parent is to make sure your child has a variety of healthy foods available when she is hungry.

A good way to learn about healthy eating is to look at the American Food Pyramid or Canada's Food Guide. The serving sizes in these guides are designed for people over four years of age, but they are a great starting point when you're deciding what foods to offer your child. Both guides focus on the four major food groups: grain products, vegetables and fruits, milk products and meat and alternatives. Each food group provides unique nutrients, so it is important to offer your child a variety of foods from each food group every day. A good rule of thumb is to aim for three of the four food groups at each meal and one or two of the food groups at each snack. This will ensure that your child gets all the nutrients she needs to grow and develop.

You can download a copy of the American Food Pyramid at **www.nal.usda.gov/fnic/Fpyr/pyramid.html**. You can download a copy of Canada's Food Guide at **http://www.hc-sc.gc.ca/fn-an/ food-guide-aliment/order-commander/index-eng.php**, or you can request one from your local public health office.

The **Dietary Reference Intake** (DRI) is the recommended daily intake of certain key nutrients, such as carbohydrates, protein, fat, calcium, vitamin C, fiber, iron and many more. These have been developed, in a joint effort by American and Canadian nutrition experts, to expand and replace the former American Recommended Dietary Allowance (RDA) and Canadian Recommended Nutrient Intake (RNI). Adequate Intake (AI) is the recommended average daily intake level. Aim to give your child this amount. The Tolerable Upper Limit (UI) is the highest average daily nutrient intake level that is likely to pose no risk of adverse health effects to almost all individuals in the general population.

Grain Products

TIP: *The term "enriched" means that a food such as white flour or white pasta has some of the vitamins added back into it after processing.*

Grain products provide most of the energy your toddler needs throughout the day. Grain products can also be a great source of fiber, vitamins and minerals, especially iron. Always choose whole grains or enriched products. Healthy examples are whole-grain or 100% whole wheat bread, high-fiber cereal and whole wheat or enriched pasta.

Nutrient Highlight: Fiber

Fiber is an essential part of a healthy diet for everyone, including infants and toddlers. Fiber is found in the cell walls of plants and is made up of a number of complex carbohydrates that cannot be digested by the body.

Fiber is essential for healthy bowel function, and a diet rich in fiber has many health benefits. We need to eat fiber foods such as grain products every day to maintain the health of our digestive systems and prevent heart disease.

Dietary Reference Intake for Fiber

0 to 6 months	Not determined
7 to 12 months	Not determined
1 to 3 years	19 g/day (AI)

There are two main types of fiber: soluble and insoluble. **Soluble fiber** is soluble in water and absorbs water like a sponge, swelling and therefore increasing the bulk of the intestines' contents. Soluble fiber can be found in such foods as apples, pears, oats, barley, psyllium, prunes and beans. Research shows that soluble fiber plays a significant role in lowering blood cholesterol levels, thereby reducing the risk of coronary heart disease. **Insoluble fiber** is not soluble in water and has the ability to speed up the rate at which food moves along the intestines. Therefore, an increase in insoluble fiber intake is recommended to help alleviate constipation. Wheat, wheat bran and seeds are excellent sources of insoluble fiber.

When choosing grain products, look for breads that have 2 grams or more fiber per slice and cereals that have more than 4 grams of fiber per serving. Good sources of fiber include whole grains, wheat bran, beans, lentils and most fruits and vegetables.

Vegetables and Fruits

Vegetables and fruits provide carbohydrate, fiber, vitamins (especially A and C) and minerals. This food group is often the most difficult for parents. Try making it fun! Use playful words such as "carrot coins" and "broccoli trees." Many of the recipes in this book combine vegetables and fruits with other food groups, which may make them more acceptable to your toddler. Most importantly, your toddler should watch you enjoying vegetables and fruits. It is not fair to expect your child to eat something you won't eat!

Dark leafy green and bright orange or red vegetables and fruits pack the most nutrients. Broccoli, spinach, squash, sweet potatoes, carrots, cantaloupe, bell peppers and berries are all great choices. Make sure that your child eats a variety of fruits and vegetables, since each offers a different combination of the vitamins and minerals essential to good health.

Nutrient Highlight: Vitamin C

The body needs vitamin C to help with healing and the development of connective tissue and healthy gums. It has been said to reduce the symptoms and duration of the common cold. Vitamin C also plays an important role in helping the body absorb iron.

Dietary Reference Intake for Vitamin C

0 to 6 months	40 mg/day (AI)
7 to 12 months	50 mg/day (AI)
1 to 3 years	15 mg/day (AI); 400 mg/day (UI)

Good sources of vitamin C include citrus fruits, tomatoes, potatoes, Brussels sprouts, cauliflower, broccoli, strawberries, cabbage, spinach and bell peppers.

Milk Products

Milk products are your child's main source of calcium and vitamin D, which are essential for strong bones and teeth. This group also provides protein, fat, vitamins and minerals. Children between 12 and 24 months of age require more fat and should therefore drink full-fat (3.5% M.F.) milk. Lower-fat 2% or 1% milk can be introduced after two years. Other healthy choices include cheese and whole-milk yogurt.

Nutrient Highlight: Calcium and Vitamin D

Calcium doesn't just help build strong bones and teeth; it is also needed for muscles such as the heart to contract, blood to clot and nerve impulses to transmit. Your bones act as a storehouse for calcium. If your calcium needs are not met through the foods you eat, it will be withdrawn from your bones.

Milk products are excellent sources of calcium. However, only fluid milk and some yogurts contain vitamin D, which helps our body absorb calcium and is equally important for bone health.

Dietary Reference Intake for Calcium

0 to 6 months	210 mg/day (AI)
7 to 12 months	270 mg/day (AI)
1 to 3 years	500 mg/day (AI)

Good sources of calcium include milk, yogurt and cheese. Good sources of vitamin D include fluid milk, egg yolks, high-fat fish and sunshine.

Meat and Alternatives

The meat and alternatives group provides a great source of protein and iron, as well as fat, vitamins and minerals. Make sure that meat is cut up into bite-size pieces, as it is sometimes hard for little teeth to chew. Healthy choices include lean beef, lamb, pork, chicken without skin and fish, especially fatty fish such as salmon.

Don't forget the alternatives! Eggs, peanut butter, tofu, beans and legumes are great sources of protein and add variety to your toddler's diet. Beans and legumes are also great sources of fiber.

Nutrient Highlight: Iron

Iron is a component of blood that helps carry oxygen. Iron deficiency is common in North America, and people who do not get enough iron can develop iron deficiency anemia. The symptoms include tiredness, irritability and loss of the ability to concentrate. Anemia can cause behavior and developmental problems in children. Iron from animal sources is called **heme iron** and is better absorbed by the body. Iron from non-animal sources is called **non-heme iron** and can be better absorbed if eaten with a food high in vitamin C.

The iron requirements of infants and children are very high. In the first six months, these iron needs are met by the stores they received from their mother during pregnancy and from breast milk or formula. After six months, these stores start to become depleted and a source of iron should be introduced. Iron-fortified infant cereal contains about 7 mg per $\frac{1}{2}$ cup (125 mL) serving. One cup (250 mL), or 8 ounces, of iron-fortified infant formula contains about 5 mg.

Dietary Reference Intake for Iron

0 to 6 months	0.27 mg/day (AI)
7 to 12 months	11 mg/day (AI)
1 to 3 years	7 mg/day (AI)

Good sources of heme iron include beef, chicken and halibut. Good sources of non-heme iron include cream of wheat cereal, iron-fortified infant cereal, spinach, potatoes, beans, legumes, enriched white rice, prune juice and whole wheat bread.

Fat

Fat provides energy and plays a role in the absorption of the fat-soluble vitamins A, D, E and K. It also provides essential fatty acids that our bodies cannot produce on their own and helps insulate our bodies, protecting our vital organs.

All types of fat have the same amount of calories, but not all fats are created equal — some are more harmful to your health than others. **Saturated fat** and **trans fat** may increase a person's risk of heart disease, and experts believe that trans fat may carry an even greater health risk than saturated fat. **Monounsaturated fat** and **polyunsaturated fat** do not have the same negative effect on the heart.

Saturated and trans fats — such as butter, shortening or the fat on meat — are solid at room temperature. Saturated fat comes mostly from animal products, but some tropical oils, such as palm kernel oil and coconut oil, also contain saturated fat. Trans fat is also found in whole dairy and meat products. But one of the most common sources of trans fat in today's foods is hydrogenated vegetable oil. Hydrogenated oils are liquid oils that have been changed into a solid form of fat by adding hydrogen. This process allows these fats to keep for a long time without losing their flavor or going bad. Trans fats are often found in packaged baked goods such as cookies, crackers and potato chips. They are also present in fried foods such as french fries and doughnuts.

Unsaturated fats are liquid at room temperature. Unsaturated fats can be polyunsaturated or monounsaturated. Polyunsaturated fat is found in soybean, corn, sesame and sunflower oils, and fish and fish oil. Monounsaturated fat is found in avocados, olives, olive oil, canola oil, and most nuts and their oils.

Dietary Reference Intake for Total Fat

0 to 6 months	31 g/day (AI)
7 to 12 months	30 g/day (AI)
1 to 3 years	Insufficient scientific evidence was found to set an AI

Salt

It is not necessary to add salt to your toddler's diet. Children are not born with the desire for salty foods; this is a learned preference. Enough salt is found naturally in foods to satisfy the body's requirement.

Sugar

Adding sugar to your child's foods masks the natural taste, which children need to learn to like. Excess sugar leads to tooth decay and many unnecessary trips to the dentist.

Dealing with a Picky Eater

It is very common for toddlers to go through stages of likes and dislikes. Remember these important points when dealing with a picky eater:

- Fussy or picky eating is a normal part of growing up.
- Don't force your child to eat. Offer him a variety of healthy choices and let him choose how much he eats. This builds confidence!
- Let your child have his favorite food of the month over and over again as long as it is a healthy choice. He will grow out of it as time goes on.

- Introduce new foods regularly, and remember that it may take up to ten attempts to get a child to try a new food.
- Be patient with your child if he seems to dawdle at the table. He is learning a lot of new skills, like using utensils and cups.
- Make sure snacks are not served too close to mealtime. A hungry child is more likely to try new foods.
- Don't become a short-order cook. Children should choose from the foods that have been prepared, not demand that a new meal be cooked for them.
- Involve your child in meal preparation. He is more likely to try a food if he helped get it to the table.
- Lead by example. Let your child see you enjoying all the healthy choices you have prepared.

If a child is fussy or picky and is not growing properly, it is time to see your doctor.

Shopping with Your Toddler

Grocery shopping with a toddler can be a nightmare for moms and dads, but, with a few strategies that involve your child, the trip can be more pleasant and maybe even enjoyable!

Try these strategies:
- Shop in the morning if you can. Toddlers tend to be grouchy near nap- or bedtimes.
- Keep your toddler strapped into the cart. This keeps your child safe and close to you. Bring wipes to clean the handle!
- Point out letters, words, numbers and colors when you shop. Count the fruit as you add it to a bag to turn your shopping trip into a learning opportunity.
- Bring a fake wallet with pretend money and credit cards for your child to play with. Your child can give you money and use a card just like mom and dad do.
- Talk about the foods you are choosing and how they will make everyone in the family healthy and strong. Let your child see how exciting and interesting food is.
- Let your child pick a few strategic healthy items; apples, bananas and grapes are good choices. When you serve them at home, remind your child who picked them out.

FOOD FOR BABIES

Six Months and Older

Continued on next page

Meal Plans

Continue breastfeeding or formula feeding on demand while you are introducing solids. Breast milk or formula is your child's best source of protein, fat and many vitamins and minerals, such as calcium. At this point, solid foods should be in addition to your regular breast milk or formula feedings. See the introduction for more information on these meal plans.

Make sure you spend time introducing your child to individual foods before introducing combination foods. This will help you identify allergies or intolerances. Please note that the amounts are just suggestions. All babies are different and require different amounts of food. Let your baby eat until he or she turns away or appears full.

MEAL plan for babies mostly formula fed

MEAL	1	2	3
Breakfast	• 2 tbsp (30 mL) prepared iron-fortified infant cereal • ¼ cup (60 mL) Apricots (page 44)	• 2 tbsp (30 mL) prepared iron-fortified infant cereal • ¼ cup (60 mL) Nectarines (page 50)	• 2 tbsp (30 mL) prepared iron-fortified infant cereal • ¼ cup (60 mL) Pears (page 52)
Snack	• Breast or formula feeding on demand	• Breast or formula feeding on demand	• Breast or formula feeding on demand
Lunch	• ¼ cup (60 mL) Sweet Potatoes (page 40)	• ¼ cup (60 mL) Squash (page 38)	• ¼ cup (60 mL) Parsnips (page 35)
Snack	• Breast or formula feeding on demand	• Breast or formula feeding on demand	• Breast or formula feeding on demand
Supper	• 2 tbsp (30 mL) prepared iron-fortified infant cereal • ¼ cup (60 mL) Apples (page 43)	• 2 tbsp (30 mL) prepared iron-fortified infant cereal • ¼ cup (60 mL) Squashed Green Beans (page 81)	• 2 tbsp (30 mL) prepared iron-fortified infant cereal • ¼ cup (60 mL) Broccoli Stems and Florets (page 28)
Snack	• Breast or formula feeding on demand	• Breast or formula feeding on demand	• Breast or formula feeding on demand

MEAL plan for babies mostly breastfed

At six months of age, iron stores your baby acquired from you during pregnancy start to decline, and an additional source of iron is required. This is particularly true for babies who are mostly breastfed, because breast milk is low in iron. Most infant formulas have been fortified with the mineral.

Meat and beans are good sources of iron and can be used as an early food, especially for babies who have been mostly breastfed. Some children have initial difficulties accepting meat products. Make sure the meats are puréed or finely minced with a little water or broth or with a vegetable.

MEAL	1	2	3
Breakfast	• 2 tbsp (30 mL) prepared iron-fortified infant cereal • ¼ cup (60 mL) Pears (page 52)	• 2 tbsp (30 mL) prepared iron-fortified infant cereal • ¼ cup (60 mL) Nectarines (page 50)	• 2 tbsp (30 mL) prepared iron-fortified infant cereal • ¼ cup (60 mL) Apricots (page 44)
Snack	• Breast or formula feeding on demand	• Breast or formula feeding on demand	• Breast or formula feeding on demand
Lunch	• ¼ cup (60 mL) Turkey (page 61)	• ¼ cup (60 mL) Squash and Split Peas (page 77)	• ¼ cup (60 mL) Lentils, Carrots, Celery (page 68)
Snack	• Breast or formula feeding on demand	• Breast or formula feeding on demand	• Breast or formula feeding on demand
Supper	• ¼ cup (60 mL) Sweet Potato Hummus (page 83)	• ¼ cup (60 mL) Chicken (page 58) • ¼ cup (60 mL) Avocado (page 45)	• ¼ cup (60 mL) Beef, Potato, Green Peas (page 97)
Snack	• Breast or formula feeding on demand	• Breast or formula feeding on demand	• Breast or formula feeding on demand

Beets

| 2 cups | chopped peeled beets (about 1 bunch) | 500 mL |
| 1/2 cup | water | 125 mL |

1. In a medium saucepan, over medium heat, bring beets and water just to a boil. Cover, reduce heat and simmer until very tender, about 20 minutes. Let cool.

2. Transfer beets to blender and purée on high speed until smooth.

**Nutritional Information
(Per 1/4-cup/60 mL Serving)**

Calories . . . . 15 Kcal
Total Carbohydrates . . . . 1 g
Fiber . . . . 1 g
Fat. . . . . 0 g
Protein . . . . 1 g
Iron. . . . . 0 mg

**MAKES ABOUT
2 CUPS (500 ML)**

Beets are very easily digested and stimulate the appetite. Be aware that beets will often discolor urine and stools, but this should not be cause for concern.

*Cooked broccoli is
an excellent source
of vitamin C and
potassium.*

TIPS

Use a vegetable peeler
to remove the fibrous
skin from broccoli
stems.

Once your baby is
used to the flavor of
broccoli, use the same
cooking method with
2½ cups (625 mL)
florets (the texture
of the buds can be
off-putting to younger
children).

Broccoli Stems and Florets

| 1½ cups | sliced peeled broccoli stems (see tips, at left) | 375 mL |
| 1 cup | water | 250 mL |

1. In a medium saucepan, over medium heat, bring
   stems and water to a boil. Cover, reduce heat
   and simmer until broccoli is very tender, about
   15 minutes. Let cool.

2. Transfer broccoli to blender and purée on high
   speed until smooth.

**Nutritional Information
(Per ¼-cup/60 mL Serving)**

Calories . . . . .8 Kcal
Total Carbohydrates . . . . .1 g
Fiber. . . . . .0 g
Fat. . . . . .0 g
Protein . . . . .1 g
Iron. . . . . 0 mg
Vitamin C . . . . 26 mg

Cabbage

3 cups	chopped cabbage (about 8 oz/250 g)	750 mL

1. Place cabbage in a steamer basket fitted over a saucepan of boiling water; cover and steam for 15 to 20 minutes, or until very tender. Let cool.

2. Transfer cabbage to blender and purée on high speed, adding water if necessary, until smooth.

**Nutritional Information
(Per ¼-cup/60 mL Serving)**

Calories	8 Kcal
Total Carbohydrates	2 g
Fiber	1 g
Fat	0 g
Protein	0 g
Iron	0 mg

**MAKES ABOUT
2 CUPS (500 ML)**

Green, red, Savoy, Napa and bok choy are some of the different varieties of this nutrient-dense vegetable. They can all be prepared in the same manner.

6

Carrots are naturally sweet and very nutritious. Cooking carrots maximizes their nutritional potential and flavor.

TIP

The green tops draw nutrients from the carrots. Choose carrots that have them removed, or remove them immediately after purchasing.

Carrots

| 2 cups | chopped peeled carrots (about 4) | 500 mL |
| 1 cup | water | 125 mL |

1. In a medium saucepan, over medium heat, bring carrots and water just to a boil. Cover, reduce heat and simmer until carrots are very tender, about 15 minutes. Let cool.

2. Transfer carrots to blender and purée on high speed until smooth.

**Nutritional Information
(Per ¼-cup/60 mL Serving)**

Calories . . . . 14 Kcal
Total Carbohydrates . . . . 3 g
Fiber . . . . 1 g
Fat . . . . 0 g
Protein . . . . 0 g
Iron . . . . 0 mg

Cauliflower

1 ½ cups	cauliflower florets	375 mL
1 cup	water	250 mL

1. In a medium saucepan, over medium heat, bring cauliflower and water just to a boil. Cover, reduce heat and simmer until cauliflower is very tender, about 10 minutes. Let cool.

2. Transfer cauliflower to blender and purée on high speed until smooth.

Nutritional Information
(Per ¼-cup/60 mL Serving)

Calories	8 Kcal
Total Carbohydrates	2 g
Fiber	1 g
Fat	0 g
Protein	0 g
Iron	0 mg

**MAKES ABOUT
2 CUPS (500 ML)**

Cauliflower is the most easily digestible member of the cabbage family and is a great introduction to the cruciferous group, which also includes cabbage, broccoli, Brussels sprouts, collard greens and kohlrabi.

TIP

Add a piece of bread to the water when boiling to absorb some of the odor. Discard bread before puréeing.

**MAKES 2 CUPS
(500 ML)**

*Purchase fresh corn still
in its husk, as it perishes
very quickly. The silk
should feel moist, and
the kernels should
be firm and should
produce a milky juice
when pierced. Shuck
the corn and remove
the kernels by running
a sharp knife along the
cob. Use immediately.*

TIP

Substitute frozen
kernels when fresh are
not in season.

Corn

| 2 cups | fresh or frozen corn kernels | 500 mL |
| 1/2 cup | water | 125 mL |

1. In a medium saucepan, over medium heat, bring corn and water just to a boil. Cover, reduce heat and simmer until corn is tender, about 3 minutes. Let cool.

2. Transfer corn to blender and purée on high speed until smooth.

**Nutritional Information
(Per 1/4-cup/60 mL Serving)**

Calories	49 Kcal
Total Carbohydrates	12 g
Fiber	1 g
Fat	0 g
Protein	2 g
Iron	0 mg

**MAKES ABOUT
1 CUP (250 ML)**

*Cucumber is very mild
and refreshing. The
waxy skin is not very
palatable for little ones,
so always peel before
using.*

MAKE AHEAD

Store in an airtight
container in the
refrigerator for up to
3 days. Do not freeze.

Cucumber

| 1 1/2 cups | cubed peeled and seeded cucumber (about 1 small) | 375 mL |

1. Place in blender and purée on high speed until smooth.

**Nutritional Information
(Per 1/4-cup/60 mL Serving)**

Calories	7 Kcal
Total Carbohydrates	2 g
Fiber	0 g
Fat	0 g
Protein	0 g
Iron	0 mg

Dark Leafy Greens

| 6 cups | chopped dark leafy greens, tough stems and ribs removed | 1.5 L |
| ½ cup | water | 125 mL |

1. Arrange greens in a large nonstick skillet. Pour in water, cover and cook over medium-high heat, stirring occasionally, until greens are very tender, about 15 minutes. Let cool.

2. Transfer greens to blender and purée on high speed, adding water if necessary, until smooth.

Nutritional Information
(Per ¼-cup/60 mL Serving)

Calories	34 Kcal
Total Carbohydrates	7 g
Fiber	1 g
Fat	0 g
Protein	2 g
Iron	1 mg
Vitamin C	80 mg

MAKES ABOUT 2 CUPS (500 ML)

Beet greens, mustard greens, kale and Swiss chard all fall into this group, and all are excellent sources of vitamin A.

Choose young green beans that are tender and not too fibrous, and remove any fibers that are on them. French beans make the smoothest purée.

TIPS

Substitute frozen green beans if fresh are not available.

If your baby is texture-sensitive, push the purée through a fine sieve with a wooden spoon to get a very smooth consistency.

Green Beans

| 3 cups | halved trimmed green beans (about 12 oz/375 g) | 750 mL |
| 2 cups | water | 500 mL |

1. In a large saucepan, over medium-high heat, bring beans and water to a boil. Cover, reduce heat and simmer until beans are very tender, about 15 minutes. Let cool.

2. Transfer beans to blender and purée on high speed until smooth.

**Nutritional Information
(Per ¼-cup/60 mL Serving)**

Calories	13 Kcal
Total Carbohydrates	3 g
Fiber	1 g
Fat	0 g
Protein	1 g
Iron	0 mg

Parsnips

2 cups	chopped peeled parsnips (about 4)	500 mL
1 cup	water	250 mL

1. In a medium saucepan, over medium heat, bring parsnips and water just to a boil. Cover, reduce heat and simmer until very tender, about 20 minutes. Let cool.

2. Transfer parsnips to blender and purée on high speed until smooth.

Nutritional Information
(Per $\frac{1}{4}$-cup/60 mL Serving)

Calories	25 Kcal
Total Carbohydrates	6 g
Fiber	2 g
Fat	0 g
Protein	0 g
Iron	0 mg

MAKES 2 CUPS (500 ML)

Like many other root vegetables, parsnips have a mild, sweet flavor that infants love.

TIP

Choose parsnips that are small and firm; larger, older parsnips have a higher starch content that may produce a purée that is too sticky once blended.

6

Pumpkin is a nice change from squash and has a flavor that babies love.

TIP

Dice extra pumpkin and freeze in a single layer on a baking sheet covered with plastic wrap. Once completely frozen, transfer to a resealable bag for use throughout the year.

Pumpkin

| 3 cups | cubed peeled pie pumpkin | 750 mL |
| 1 cup | water | 250 mL |

1. In a large saucepan, over medium-high heat, bring pumpkin and water to a boil. Cover, reduce heat and simmer until pumpkin is very tender, about 25 minutes. Let cool.

2. Transfer pumpkin and cooking liquid to blender and purée on high speed until smooth.

**Nutritional Information
(Per ¼-cup/60 mL Serving)**

Calories . . . . 8 Kcal
Total Carbohydrates . . . . 2 g
Fiber . . . . 0 g
Fat . . . . 0 g
Protein . . . . 0 g
Iron . . . . 0 mg

Spinach

4 cups	lightly packed fresh spinach leaves (about 3 oz/90 g)	1 L
½ cup	water	125 mL

1. Wash spinach leaves thoroughly in a basin of cold water, changing water often. Remove tough stems and ribs and roughly chop leaves.

2. Arrange spinach in a large nonstick skillet. Pour in water, cover and cook over medium-high heat, stirring occasionally, until wilted and bright green, about 5 minutes. Let cool.

3. Transfer spinach to blender and purée on high speed until smooth.

Nutritional Information
(Per ¼-cup/60 mL Serving)

Calories	3 Kcal
Total Carbohydrates	1 g
Fiber	0 g
Fat	0 g
Protein	0 g
Iron	0 mg

**MAKES ABOUT
2 CUPS (500 ML)**

Wash spinach very well and don't overcook it — overcooking can bring out its bitterness. Old, tough leaves should be avoided.

TIPS

Substitute frozen spinach when fresh is not available.

Spinach can also be used raw if using tender baby spinach leaves.

6

*In autumn, any variety
of squash makes an
ideal beginner purée.*

TIP

Use diced frozen
squash when fresh is
not in season or when
you're in a hurry.

Squash

| 3 cups | cubed peeled butternut or acorn squash | 750 mL |
| 1 cup | water | 250 mL |

1. In a medium saucepan, over medium-high heat, bring squash and water to a boil. Cover, reduce heat and simmer until squash is very tender, about 20 minutes. Let cool.

2. Transfer squash to blender and purée on high speed until smooth.

**Nutritional Information
(Per ¼-cup/60 mL Serving)**

Calories . . . . 12 Kcal
Total Carbohydrates . . . . 3 g
Fiber . . . . 0 g
Fat . . . . 0 g
Protein . . . . 0 g
Iron . . . . 0 mg

Sweet Peas

| 3 cups | fresh or frozen sweet peas | 750 mL |
| 2 cups | water | 500 mL |

1. In a large saucepan, over medium-high heat, bring peas and water to a boil. Cover, reduce heat and simmer for 5 minutes, until peas are tender. Let cool.

2. Transfer peas to blender and purée on high speed until smooth.

**Nutritional Information
(Per ¼-cup/60 mL Serving)**

Calories	42 Kcal
Total Carbohydrates	7 g
Fiber	3 g
Fat	0 g
Protein	3 g
Iron	1 mg

**MAKES ABOUT
2 CUPS (500 ML)**

If shelling peas isn't quite the labor of love you were looking for, frozen peas offer the same nutritional value without the work.

TIP

If your baby is texture-sensitive, push the purée through a fine sieve with a wooden spoon to get a very smooth consistency.

Sweet potatoes, carrots, mangoes and other orange fruits and vegetables are high in beta carotene, which the body converts to vitamin A. Vitamin A is important for vision, bone growth, reproduction and cell division.

Sweet Potatoes

| 3 cups | cubed peeled sweet potatoes (about 2) | 750 mL |
| 1 cup | water | 250 mL |

1. In a medium saucepan, over medium-high heat, bring potatoes and water to a boil. Cover, reduce heat and simmer until potatoes are very tender, about 20 minutes. Let cool.

2. Transfer potatoes to blender and purée on high speed until smooth.

**Nutritional Information
(Per $\frac{1}{4}$-cup/60 mL Serving)**

Calories . . . . 26 Kcal
Total Carbohydrates . . . . 6 g
Fiber . . . . 1 g
Fat . . . . 0 g
Protein . . . . 0 g
Iron . . . . 0 mg

Turnips

| 2 cups | chopped peeled white turnips (about 4) | 500 mL |
| 1 cup | water | 250 mL |

1. In a medium saucepan, over medium-high heat, bring turnips and water to a boil. Cover, reduce heat and simmer until turnips are very tender, about 15 minutes. Let cool.

2. Transfer turnips to blender and purée on high speed until smooth.

Nutritional Information
(Per ¼-cup/60 mL Serving)

Calories	9 Kcal
Total Carbohydrates	2 g
Fiber	1 g
Fat	0 g
Protein	0 g
Iron	0 mg

MAKES ABOUT 2 CUPS (500 ML)

Turnips are purplish white root vegetables that are similar in size to beets. In North America, we often refer to rutabagas as turnips, but rutabagas are large, yellow-fleshed, waxy vegetables that are harder on babies' stomachs.

Choose zucchini and yellow squash that are small and have thin, unblemished skin; they are the most tender and have a sweet mild flavor.

TIP

Scrub zucchini well and cut off both ends, but do not peel: the rind offers both nutrients and a delightful pale green color!

Zucchini/Yellow Squash

3 cups	sliced zucchini or yellow squash (about 2)	750 mL

1. Place zucchini in a steaming basket fitted over a saucepan of boiling water, cover and steam for 15 minutes, or until very tender. Let cool.

2. Transfer zucchini to blender and purée on high speed until smooth.

**Nutritional Information
(Per ¼-cup/60 mL Serving)**

Calories	5 Kcal
Total Carbohydrates	1 g
Fiber	0 g
Fat	0 g
Protein	0 g
Iron	0 mg

Apples

4 cups	chopped peeled apples (about 4)	1 L
½ cup	water	125 mL

1. In a medium saucepan, over medium-low heat, bring apples and water to a simmer, covered, stirring occasionally, until apples are very tender, about 20 minutes.

2. Transfer apples to blender and purée on high speed until smooth.

Nutritional Information
(Per ¼-cup/60 mL Serving)

Calories	12 Kcal
Total Carbohydrates	3 g
Fiber	1 g
Fat	0 g
Protein	0 g
Iron	0 mg

**MAKES ABOUT
2 CUPS (500 ML)**

Apples are a good source of soluble fiber, which helps with bowel function and may lower cholesterol levels.

**MAKES ABOUT
2 CUPS (500 ML)**

*Apricots are very
high in beta carotene
and are an appetite
stimulant. They have
a stronger flavor than
peaches and nectarines,
so you may choose to
dilute this purée with
a bit of infant cereal
when you first try it.
If you're using dried
apricots, be aware
that they have mild
laxative qualities.*

TIP

Substitute dried
apricots when fresh
are not in season. Look
for apricots that have
not been treated with
sulfites. Use 2 dried
for each fresh apricot.
Place dried apricots
in a bowl and pour in
boiling water to cover.
Let sit for 30 minutes
to rehydrate. Drain
and blend according
to recipe.

Apricots

| 2 cups | apricots | 500 mL |
| 1/4 cup | water | 60 mL |

1. In a small saucepan of boiling water, blanch apricots for 30 seconds. Remove stones from apricots and chop.

2. Place in blender with 1/4 cup (60 mL) water and purée on high speed until smooth.

**Nutritional Information
(Per 1/4-cup/60 mL Serving)**

Calories . . . . 18 Kcal
Total Carbohydrates . . . . 4 g
Fiber . . . . 1 g
Fat . . . . 0 g
Protein . . . . 0 g
Iron . . . . 0 mg

Avocado

| 1/4 cup | chopped peeled avocado (about 1/2) | 60 mL |

1. Place avocado in blender and purée on high speed until smooth.

Nutritional Information (Per 1/4-cup/60 mL Serving)	
Calories . . . . .59 Kcal
Total Carbohydrates . . . . .3 g
Fiber . . . . .1 g
Fat. . . . . .6 g
Protein . . . . .1 g
Iron. . . . . .0 mg

MAKES ABOUT 1/4 CUP (60 ML)

Avocado provides essential fats for proper growth and has a buttery texture that babies love!

TIP

Avocados turn gray very quickly after slicing — use up this purée as soon as it's made.

Banana

| 1 | very ripe banana | 1 |

1. Place banana in blender and purée on high speed until smooth.

2. *Make ahead:* Store in an airtight container in the refrigerator for up to 1 day.

Nutritional Information (Per 1/4-cup/60 mL Serving)	
Calories . . . . .80 Kcal
Total Carbohydrates .20 g
Fiber . . . . .2 g
Fat. . . . . .0 g
Protein . . . . .1 g
Iron. . . . . .0 mg

MAKES ABOUT 1/2 CUP (125 ML)

This "peel and mash" fruit is always quick, convenient and nutritious. Bananas are high in potassium and vitamin B$_6$.

TIP

Freeze chunks of unblemished bananas on a baking sheet in a single layer. When frozen, transfer to a resealable bag and freeze for up to 6 months. Purée until smooth to make a frozen banana treat.

Blueberries are fine to purée on high speed without cooking, but tend to be more tart that way.

TIP

Make up a batch of this recipe and blend a frozen cube of it (see introduction, page 14) with any fruit favorite, such as apples, pears or bananas.

Blueberries

| 2 cups | blueberries (about 12 oz/375 g) | 500 mL |
| 1/2 cup | water | 125 mL |

1. In a medium saucepan, over medium heat, bring blueberries and water just to a boil. Cover, reduce heat and simmer for 15 minutes, until berries are very tender. Let cool.

2. Transfer blueberries to blender and purée on high speed until smooth.

3. Push through a fine sieve with a wooden spoon to remove any seeds that may be offensive to your baby.

**Nutritional Information
(Per 1/4-cup/60 mL Serving)**

Calories	20 Kcal
Total Carbohydrates	5 g
Fiber	1 g
Fat	0 g
Protein	0 g
Iron	0 mg

Cherries

| 2 cups | pitted sweet red or black cherries (about 1 lb/500 g) | 500 mL |

1. Place cherries in blender and purée on high speed until smooth.

Nutritional Information (Per ¼-cup/60 mL Serving)

Calories	18 Kcal
Total Carbohydrates	4 g
Fiber	1 g
Fat	0 g
Protein	0 g
Iron	0 mg

MAKES 2 CUPS (500 ML)

Summer sweet cherries are the ultimate treat!

TIP

Cherries can be purchased already pitted and chilled, and can be portioned out and frozen to enjoy all year long.

Figs

| 2 cups | black figs, stems removed (about 8 oz/250 g) | 500 mL |
| ½ cup | water | 125 mL |

1. In a medium saucepan, over medium heat, bring figs and water just to a boil. Cover, reduce heat and simmer until figs are very tender, about 15 minutes. Let cool.

2. Transfer figs to blender and purée on high speed until smooth.

Nutritional Information (Per ¼-cup/60 mL Serving)

Calories	37 Kcal
Total Carbohydrates	10 g
Fiber	2 g
Fat	0 g
Protein	0 g
Iron	0 mg

MAKES ABOUT 2 CUPS (500 ML)

Fresh figs are a good source of potassium and fiber; they also tend to have laxative properties.

TIP

If your baby is texture-sensitive, push the purée through a fine sieve with a wooden spoon to get a very smooth consistency.

*Kiwis are high in
vitamins C and E and
act as antioxidants.
They have a rich,
buttery texture that
appeals to babies.*

TIP

Choose kiwis that are
firm but yield to gentle
pressure. Place them
in a brown paper bag
to ripen.

Kiwi

| 3 cups | chopped peeled kiwis (about 6) | 750 mL |

1. Place kiwis in blender and purée on high speed
until smooth.

2. *Make ahead:* Store in an airtight container in the
refrigerator for up to 3 days. Do not freeze.

| **Nutritional Information** |
| **(Per ¼-cup/60 mL Serving)** |
| Calories . . . . 27 Kcal |
| Total Carbohydrates . . . . 7 g |
| Fiber . . . . 1 g |
| Fat . . . . 0 g |
| Protein . . . . 0 g |
| Iron . . . . 0 mg |
| Vitamin C . . . . 43 mg |

Orange Pumpkin Purée (page 69) and
Squashed Vegetable Purée (page 78)

Chicken Stew (page 98)

Citrus Couscous (page 114)

Dhal for Beginners (page 115)

Mango

| 3 cups | chopped peeled mangoes (about 2 large) | 750 mL |
| ¼ cup | water | 60 mL |

1. Place mangoes and water in blender and purée on high speed until smooth.

**Nutritional Information
(Per ¼-cup/60 mL Serving)**

Calories	27 Kcal
Total Carbohydrates	7 g
Fiber	1 g
Fat	0 g
Protein	0 g
Iron	0 mg

Mangoes help the body maintain bowel regularity and fight infection. The skin can irritate a baby's mouth, so always peel.

TIP

Mangoes should have unblemished red and yellow skin that yields slightly to pressure. If mango is very fibrous, push puréed mango through a fine sieve to give a smooth, creamy consistency.

Melon

| 3 cups | cubed cantaloupe or honeydew melon (about ½) | 750 mL |

1. Place melon chunks in blender and purée on high speed until smooth.

**Nutritional Information
(Per ¼-cup/60 mL Serving)**

Calories	5 Kcal
Total Carbohydrates	1 g
Fiber	0 g
Fat	0 g
Protein	0 g
Iron	0 mg

Melons are a good source of vitamin A and contain vitamin C and calcium. They have a mild, sweet flavor that appeals to babies.

TIP

Choose melons that are unblemished and heavy for their size and give off a fruity fragrance.

Nectarines

Nectarines should be heavy, firm, but not hard, with patches of red.

TIP

If you prefer to peel nectarines before puréeing, blanch them in boiling water for 30 seconds and transfer immediately to ice water. The peel will then come off easily.

| 3 cups | chopped nectarines (about 4) | 750 mL |
| 1/4 cup | water | 60 mL |

1. Place nectarines and water in blender and purée on high speed until smooth.

**Nutritional Information
(Per 1/4-cup/60 mL Serving)**

Calories	17 Kcal
Total Carbohydrates	4 g
Fiber	1 g
Fat	0 g
Protein	0 g
Iron	0 mg

Papaya

**MAKES ABOUT
2 CUPS (500 ML)**

Papaya is an excellent source of vitamin C and a good source of potassium and vitamin A.

TIP

Avoid papayas that are hard and green: they will be flavorless and will never ripen.

| 3 cups | chopped peeled papaya (about 2) | 750 mL |
| 1/4 cup | water | 60 mL |

1. Place papaya and water in blender and purée on high speed until smooth.

**Nutritional Information
(Per 1/4-cup/60 mL Serving)**

Calories	20 Kcal
Total Carbohydrates	5 g
Fiber	1 g
Fat	0 g
Protein	0 g
Iron	0 mg
Vitamin C	32 mg

Peaches

| 4 | peaches | 4 |
| ½ cup | water | 125 mL |

1. In a small saucepan of boiling water, blanch peaches for 30 seconds. Plunge into cold water. Remove peel and stones from peaches and chop to make about 3 cups (750 mL).

2. Place in blender, add water and purée on high speed until smooth.

**Nutritional Information
(Per ¼-cup/60 mL Serving)**

Calories	18 Kcal
Total Carbohydrates	5 g
Fiber	1 g
Fat	0 g
Protein	0 g
Iron	0 mg

Peaches spoil very easily, even when unripe, so buy only the quantity you are going to use and handle them with care, as they bruise easily. Store at room temperature until ready to use.

TIP

Substitute 3 cups (750 mL) frozen unsweetened sliced peaches if fresh are not available.

*Pears are a sweet source
of soluble fiber.*

TIP

Very ripe pears can be
washed, peeled, cored,
chopped and processed
in the blender without
cooking.

Pears

| 3 cups | chopped peeled pears (about 4) | 750 mL |
| 1/2 cup | water | 125 mL |

1. In a medium saucepan, over medium-low heat,
   bring pears and water to a simmer, covered, stirring
   occasionally, until pears are very tender, about
   20 minutes. Let cool.

2. Transfer pears to blender and purée on high speed
   until smooth.

**Nutritional Information
(Per 1/4-cup/60 mL Serving)**

Calories	24 Kcal
Total Carbohydrates	6 g
Fiber	1 g
Fat	0 g
Protein	0 g
Iron	0 mg

Plums

| 3 cups | chopped plums (about 6) | 750 mL |
| ½ cup | water | 125 mL |

1. In a medium saucepan, over medium-low heat, bring plums and water to a simmer, covered, stirring occasionally, until plums are very tender, about 20 minutes. Let cool.

2. Transfer plums to blender and purée on high speed until smooth.

**Nutritional Information
(Per ¼-cup/60 mL Serving)**

Calories	23 Kcal
Total Carbohydrates	5 g
Fiber	1 g
Fat	0 g
Protein	0 g
Iron	0 mg

**MAKES ABOUT
2 CUPS (500 ML)**

Like prunes and apricots, plums have laxative properties. They are excellent stewed, as in this recipe, or puréed fresh when they are ripe and sweet.

TIP

Look for plums with a powdery "bloom" on them; it's a sign that they haven't been handled too much.

*These natural laxatives
should be used in
moderation unless
constipation is an issue.*

TIP

If your baby is
texture-sensitive,
push the purée
through a fine sieve
with a wooden spoon
to get a very smooth
consistency.

Prunes

1 1/2 cups	pitted prunes (about 8 oz/250 g)	375 mL
1/2 cup	water	125 mL

1. In a medium saucepan, over medium heat, bring
prunes and water just to a boil. Cover, reduce heat
and simmer until prunes are very tender, about
15 minutes. Let cool.

2. Transfer prunes to blender and purée on high speed
until smooth.

Nutritional Information (Per 1/4-cup/60 mL Serving)	
Calories	75 Kcal
Total Carbohydrates	20 g
Fiber	2 g
Fat	0 g
Protein	1 g
Iron	0 mg

Strawberries, Raspberries or Blackberries

| 2 cups | fresh raspberries, blackberries or sliced strawberries | 500 mL |
| 1/2 cup | water | 125 mL |

1. Place berries and water in blender and purée on high speed until smooth.

2. Push through a fine sieve with a wooden spoon to remove any seeds.

MAKES ABOUT 2 CUPS (500 ML)

Berries are sometimes hard on little tummies. Try berries when baby has tried many of the other fruits and vegetables and the digestive tract is more developed. Make sure to watch for a reaction.

TIP

Use an equal amount of frozen berries when fresh are not in season.

Nutritional Information (Per 1/4-cup/60 mL Serving)

Raspberries
Calories . . . . 16 Kcal
Total Carbohydrates . . . . 4 g
Fiber . . . . 2 g
Fat . . . . 0 g
Protein . . . . 0 g
Iron . . . . 0 mg

Blackberries
Calories . . . . 19 Kcal
Total Carbohydrates . . . . 5 g
Fiber . . . . 2 g
Fat . . . . 0 g
Protein . . . . 0 g
Iron . . . . 0 mg

Strawberries
Calories . . . . 11 Kcal
Total Carbohydrates . . . . 3 g
Fiber . . . . 1 g
Fat . . . . 0 g
Protein . . . . 0 g
Iron . . . . 0 mg
Vitamin C . . . . 21 mg

*The high water content
of melons makes them
very refreshing for
little palates.*

Watermelon

2½ cups   chopped seedless watermelon   375 mL

1. Place watermelon in blender and purée on high
speed until smooth.

Nutritional Information (Per ¼-cup/60 mL Serving)	
Calories	15 Kcal
Total Carbohydrates	3 g
Fiber	0 g
Fat	0 g
Protein	0 g
Iron	0 mg

Beef

8 oz	lean ground sirloin beef	250 g
1 cup	water	250 mL

1. In a skillet, brown beef over medium-high heat, breaking up any large pieces, until no longer pink, about 7 minutes. Drain and let cool.

2. Transfer to blender, add water and purée on high speed until smooth.

**Nutritional Information
(Per ¼-cup/60 mL Serving)**

Calories	115 Kcal
Total Carbohydrates	0 g
Fiber	0 g
Fat	8 g
Protein	10 g
Iron	1 mg

**MAKES ABOUT
2 CUPS (500 ML)**

TIP

For better flavor, substitute an equal amount of homemade beef stock (see page 63) for the water.

**MAKES ABOUT
1½ CUPS (375 ML)**

TIPS

Roasted or poached chicken can be blended in the same manner.

For better flavor, substitute an equal amount of homemade chicken stock (see page 62) for the water.

Chicken

| 8 oz | boneless skinless chicken breast, cut in strips | 250 g |
| 1 cup | water | 250 mL |

1. Arrange chicken in a steamer basket fitted over a saucepan of boiling water. Cover and steam until chicken is no longer pink inside, about 20 minutes. Let cool.

2. Transfer to blender, add water and purée on high speed to desired consistency.

**Nutritional Information
(Per ¼-cup/60 mL Serving)**

Calories . . . . 50 Kcal
Total Carbohydrates . . . . 0 g
Fiber . . . . 0 g
Fat . . . . 1 g
Protein . . . . 10 g
Iron . . . . 1 mg

Lentils

**MAKES ABOUT
2 CUPS (500 ML)**

1 cup	dry red or green lentils, rinsed	250 mL
½ cup	grated carrot	125 mL
2 cups	water or homemade vegetable stock	500 mL

1. In a saucepan, over medium-high heat, bring lentils, carrot and water to a boil. Reduce heat, cover and simmer for about 15 minutes or until most of the liquid has been absorbed. Let cool slightly.

2. Transfer to blender, purée on high speed until smooth.

Lentils provide slow-burning, complex carbohydrates and replenish iron stores. They are also a great source of protein.

**Nutritional Information
(Per ¼-cup/60 mL Serving)**

Calories	82 Kcal
Total Carbohydrates	14 g
Fiber	4 g
Fat	0 g
Protein	6 g
Iron	1.3 mg

MAKES ABOUT
2 CUPS (500 ML)

*Use lean cuts of pork
that have not been
salted or cured. Avoid
bacon, sausages and
deli meats — they
have too much sodium
and nitrates for little
digestive systems.*

Pork

| 8 oz | pork tenderloin, diced | 250 g |
| 1 cup | water | 250 mL |

1. In a medium saucepan, over medium heat, bring pork and water just to a boil. Cover, reduce heat and simmer until pork is no longer pink inside, about 15 minutes. Let cool.

2. Transfer to blender and purée on high speed until smooth.

**Nutritional Information
(Per ¼-cup/60 mL Serving)**

Calories . . . . 68 Kcal
Total Carbohydrates . . . . .0 g
Fiber . . . . .0 g
Fat . . . . .2 g
Protein . . . . .12 g
Iron . . . . 1 mg

Turkey

8 oz	boneless turkey, chopped	250 g
1 cup	water	250 mL

1. Arrange turkey in a steamer basket fitted over a saucepan of boiling water. Cover and steam until turkey is no longer pink, about 20 minutes. Let cool.

2. Transfer to blender, add water and purée on high speed until desired consistency.

**Nutritional Information
(Per ¼-cup/60 mL Serving)**

Calories	40 Kcal
Total Carbohydrates	0 g
Fiber	0 g
Fat	0.2 g
Protein	9 g
Iron	0.5 mg

**MAKES ABOUT
1½ CUPS (375 ML)**

This inexpensive lean poultry is lower in fat than most proteins and offers a great, mild flavor babies love.

Homemade stock ensures that the ingredients are fresh and no salt is added.

TIP

Stock can be stored in the refrigerator for up to 5 days or portioned and frozen for up to 3 months.

Homemade Stock
(Vegetable, Chicken and Beef)

Vegetable Stock

1	large onion, diced	1
1	carrot, peeled and diced	1
1	celery stalk, diced	1
1	bay leaf	1
2	sprigs thyme	2
6 cups	water	1.5 L

1. In a large saucepan, bring onion, carrot, celery, bay leaf, thyme and water to a boil. Reduce heat and simmer, uncovered, for 60 minutes.

2. Remove from heat, cover and let cool completely.

3. Strain through sieve into a sealable container.

Chicken Stock

2 cups	chicken bones	500 mL
1	large onion, diced	1
1	carrot, peeled and diced	1
1	celery stalk, diced	1
1	bay leaf	1
2	sprigs thyme	2
6 cups	water	1.5 L

1. In a large saucepan, bring chicken bones, onion, carrot, celery, bay leaf, thyme and water to a boil. Reduce heat and simmer, uncovered, for 60 minutes.

2. Remove from heat, cover and let cool completely.

3. Strain through sieve into a sealable container.

Beef Stock

2 cups	beef bones	500 mL
1	large onion, diced	1
1	carrot, peeled and diced	1
1	celery stalk, diced	1
2 tsp	olive oil	10 mL
1	bay leaf	1
2	sprigs thyme	2
6 cups	water	1.5 L

1. Toss beef bones, onion, carrots and celery in olive oil to coat. Arrange in a single layer on a baking sheet and roast in a 400°F (200°C) oven, turning once, until bones and vegetables are roasted and well browned, about 30 minutes.

2. Transfer bones and vegetables to a large saucepan; add bay leaf, thyme and water. Bring to a boil, reduce heat and simmer for 60 minutes.

3. Remove from heat, cover and cool completely.

4. Strain through sieve into a sealable container.

**MAKES ABOUT
2 CUPS (500 ML)**

TIP

Use an equal amount of frozen raspberries when fresh are not in season.

Carrots with Apricots and Berries

1 cup	diced peeled carrots (about 2)	250 mL
1 cup	sliced pitted apricots (2 to 3)	250 mL
½ cup	raspberries	125 mL

1. Place carrots in a steaming basket fitted over a saucepan of boiling water; cover and steam until very tender, about 15 minutes. Let cool.

2. In blender, combine carrots, apricots and raspberries; purée on high speed until smooth. Pass through a fine sieve with a wooden spoon to remove seeds.

Nutritional Information (Per ¼-cup/60 mL Serving)	
Calories	20 Kcal
Total Carbohydrates	5 g
Fiber	1 g
Fat	0 g
Protein	1 g
Iron	0 mg

Carrots and Dates

2 cups	sliced peeled carrots (about 4)	500 mL
1 cup	unsweetened apple juice or water	250 mL
½ cup	chopped pitted dates (about 3 oz/90 g)	125 mL

1. In a medium saucepan, over medium-high heat, bring carrots, apple juice and dates to a boil. Cover, reduce heat and simmer until carrots are very tender, about 15 minutes. Let cool.

2. Transfer to blender and purée on high speed until smooth.

Nutritional Information
(Per ¼-cup/60 mL Serving)

Calories . . . . 52 Kcal
Total Carbohydrates . . . . 13 g
Fiber . . . . 1 g
Fat . . . . 0 g
Protein . . . . 0 g
Iron . . . . 0 mg

**MAKES ABOUT
2 CUPS (500 ML)**

Dates lend sweetness and fiber to a favorite vegetable!

TIP

Use this as a spread on whole-grain toast and bran muffins for the whole family.

*Sweet and mild root
vegetables team up
in this tasty purée!*

TIP

Choose parsnips that
are small and firm;
larger, older parsnips
have a higher starch
content that may
produce a purée that
is too sticky once
blended.

VARIATION

Substitute an equal
amount of chopped
celery for the celery
root.

Celery Root, Carrots and Parsnips

1 cup	cubed peeled carrots (about 2)	250 mL
½ cup	cubed peeled celery root	125 mL
½ cup	cubed peeled parsnip (about 1)	125 mL

1. In a medium saucepan, over medium-high heat, combine carrots, celery root and parsnip. Pour in enough water just to cover. Bring to a boil. Cover, reduce heat and simmer until all vegetables are very tender, about 15 minutes. Let cool.

2. Transfer to blender with cooking liquid and purée on high speed until smooth.

**Nutritional Information
(Per ¼-cup/60 mL Serving)**

Calories	14 Kcal
Total Carbohydrates	3 g
Fiber	1 g
Fat	0 g
Protein	0 g
Iron	0 mg

Corny Sweet Potatoes

1 ½ cups	diced peeled sweet potato (about 1)	500 mL
1 cup	corn kernels	250 mL
¼ cup	orange juice	60 mL
1 tbsp	blackstrap molasses	15 mL

1. Place sweet potato in a steaming basket fitted over a saucepan of boiling water. Cover and steam until very tender, about 20 minutes. Add corn and steam for 2 minutes longer. Let cool.

2. Transfer sweet potato and corn to blender and add orange juice and molasses; purée on high speed until smooth.

Nutritional Information
(Per ¼-cup/60 mL Serving)

Calories	53 Kcal
Total Carbohydrates	12 g
Fiber	1 g
Fat	0 g
Protein	1 g
Iron	0 mg

**MAKES ABOUT
2 CUPS (500 ML)**

Molasses adds iron and a hint of sweetness to two favorites.

TIPS

There are many types of molasses available, but blackstrap has the least amount of sugar and the most nutrients.

Sweet potatoes are a good source of beta carotene.

**MAKES ABOUT
2 CUPS (500 ML)**

Lentils are an excellent source of folic acid and potassium. Adding lentils to boiling liquid makes them easier for the baby to digest. Mixed with rice, this makes a complete meal.

TIP

Lentils do not have to be soaked, but rinse well in a sieve and pick through to remove any small stones.

VARIATION

Substitute an equal amount of red lentils for the green lentils and decrease the cooking time in Step 2 to 10 minutes.

Lentils, Carrots and Celery

1 tbsp	vegetable oil	15 mL
½ cup	chopped onion	125 mL
½ cup	chopped carrot	125 mL
½ cup	chopped celery	125 mL
2 cups	water or homemade vegetable stock	500 mL
1 cup	dried green lentils, rinsed	250 mL

1. In a medium saucepan, heat oil over medium-high heat. Add onion, carrot and celery and cook, stirring occasionally, until tender but not browned, about 5 minutes.

2. Add water and lentils; cover, reduce heat and simmer until lentils are tender, about 30 minutes. Let cool.

3. Transfer to blender and purée on high speed until smooth.

**Nutritional Information
(Per ½-cup/125 mL Serving)**

Calories . . . . 117 Kcal
Total Carbohydrates . . . . 16 g
Fiber . . . . 9 g
Fat . . . . 2 g
Protein . . . . 10 g
Iron . . . . 3 mg

Orange Pumpkin Purée

**MAKES ABOUT
2 CUPS (500 ML)**

Preheat oven to 350°F (180°C)
Rimmed baking sheet, lined with foil

2 cups	cubed peeled pie pumpkin	500 mL
1 tbsp	vegetable oil	15 mL
1 tsp	ground cinnamon	5 mL
Pinch	ground allspice	Pinch
½ cup	orange juice	125 mL

Pumpkin has more flavor than other varieties of winter squash; it's a nice alternative when in season.

1. In a medium bowl, toss pumpkin with vegetable oil, cinnamon and allspice.

2. Arrange in a single layer on prepared baking sheet and bake in preheated oven until pumpkin is golden and tender, about 30 minutes. Let cool slightly.

3. Transfer to blender, add orange juice and purée on high speed until smooth.

TIPS

Do not substitute canned pie filling, which has additives in it, for the pumpkin.

Cut peeled and seeded pumpkin into chunks and freeze in a resealable bag for up to 6 months.

**Nutritional Information
(Per ¼-cup/60 mL Serving)**

Calories	30 Kcal
Total Carbohydrates	4 g
Fiber	0 g
Fat	2 g
Protein	0 g
Iron	0 mg

6

*Combining fruits and
veggies is a great way
to pack nutrients into
simple purées.*

Pears, Carrots and Squash

1 cup	diced peeled butternut squash	250 mL
1 ½ cup	sliced peeled pear (about 1)	250 mL
½ cup	sliced peeled carrot (about 1)	125 mL
¼ cup	unsweetened apple juice or water	60 mL

1. In a medium saucepan, over medium heat, combine squash, pear, carrot and apple juice. Bring to a simmer, cover and cook until all are very tender, about 20 minutes. Let cool.

2. Transfer to blender and purée on high speed until smooth.

**Nutritional Information
(Per ¼-cup/60 mL Serving)**

Calories	24 Kcal
Total Carbohydrates	6 g
Fiber	1 g
Fat	0 g
Protein	0 g
Iron	0 mg

Pumped-Up Potatoes

**MAKES ABOUT
2 CUPS (500 ML)**

1 cup	diced peeled potatoes	250 mL
2 cups	water or homemade vegetable stock	500 mL
1/2 cup	chopped kale	125 mL
1/4 cup	iron-fortified infant cereal	60 mL

Sneak in extra nutrients whenever possible! The bitterness of kale is completely mellowed by creamy potatoes and fortified with a little cereal.

1. In a small saucepan, combine potatoes and water over medium-high heat. Bring to a boil and reduce heat. Simmer 15 minutes or until potatoes are tender. Add kale and cook 5 more minutes. Stir in cereal.

2. Transfer to blender and purée on high speed until smooth.

**Nutritional Information
(Per 1/4-cup/60 mL Serving)**

Calories	26 Kcal
Total Carbohydrates	6 g
Fiber	0.5 g
Fat	0.1 g
Protein	0.7 g
Iron	1 mg

6

**MAKES ABOUT
2 CUPS (500 ML)**

These two fall favorites have mild, slightly sweet flavors that taste great together.

TIP

Pie pumpkins are sold in the autumn and usually weigh 1 to 3 lbs (500 g to 1.5 kg). They have a sweeter flavor and are less fibrous than the larger varieties sold for carving.

Pumpkin and Apples

2 cups	cubed peeled apples (about 2)	500 mL
1 cup	diced peeled pie pumpkin	250 mL
½ cup	unsweetened apple juice	125 mL
1 tsp	vanilla	5 mL
½ tsp	ground cinnamon	2 mL

1. In a medium saucepan, over medium-low heat, combine apples, pumpkin, apple juice, vanilla and cinnamon. Cover and simmer until apples and pumpkin are very tender, about 30 minutes. Let cool.

2. Transfer to blender and purée on high speed until smooth.

Nutritional Information (Per ¼-cup/60 mL Serving)	
Calories	22 Kcal
Total Carbohydrates	5 g
Fiber	1 g
Fat	0 g
Protein	1 g
Iron	0 mg

Purple Pears

1 cup	diced peeled beets (about 2)	250 mL
1 cup	diced peeled pear (about 1)	250 mL
½ cup	unsweetened apple juice	125 mL

1. In a medium saucepan, over low heat, combine beets, pear and apple juice. Bring to a simmer, cover and cook until beets and pears are very tender, about 30 minutes. Let cool.

2. Transfer to blender with cooking liquid and purée on high speed until smooth.

**Nutritional Information
(Per ¼-cup/60 mL Serving)**

Calories	27 Kcal
Total Carbohydrates	7 g
Fiber	1 g
Fat	0 g
Protein	0 g
Iron	0 mg

**MAKES ABOUT
2 CUPS (500 ML)**

The color alone makes this worth making! This smooth, deep purple purée is sure to be a hit and will be added to your baby's growing repertoire of veggie favorites. Be aware that beets will often discolor urine and stools, but this is not a cause for concern.

TIPS

Avoid buying elongated beets — they are more fibrous and do not provide a smooth-textured purée.

Use gloves when peeling beets so you don't stain your hands (but lemon juice does the trick in removing the stains if you forget).

*Red lentils provide a
sweet, delicate flavor
and combine with
creamy banana to
provide a protein-rich
meal for little tummies.*

Red Lentils and Bananas

1/2 cup	dry red lentils, rinsed	125 mL
1 cup	water or rice beverage	250 mL
1/2 cup	chopped banana	125 mL
Pinch	cinnamon (optional)	Pinch

1. In a small saucepan, combine lentils and water. Bring to a boil over medium-high heat. Reduce heat, cover and simmer about 10 minutes or until most of the liquid has been absorbed. Let cool slightly.

2. Transfer to blender with banana and cinnamon; purée on high speed until smooth, adding more water if necessary.

**Nutritional Information
(Per 1/4-cup/60 mL Serving)**

Calories . . . . 92 Kcal
Total Carbohydrates . . . . 16 g
Fiber . . . . 4 g
Fat . . . . 0.5 g
Protein . . . . 7 g
Iron . . . . 1.4 mg

Red Pepper and White Bean Soup

½ cup	white beans, rinsed and drained	125 mL
½ cup	chopped red bell pepper	125 mL
1½ cups	water or homemade vegetable stock	375 mL

1. In a saucepan, combine beans, red pepper and water. Cook over medium heat about 8 minutes or until peppers are soft. Let cool slightly.

2. Transfer to blender and purée on high speed until smooth.

**Nutritional Information
(Per ¼-cup/60 mL Serving)**

Calories	16 Kcal
Total Carbohydrates	3 g
Fiber	1 g
Fat	0 g
Protein	1 g
Iron	0.2 mg

**MAKES ABOUT
2 CUPS (500 ML)**

White beans provide great texture and fiber in this rich "creamy" soup.

*This silky-smooth
purée just might
convert babies who
don't like squash!*

TIP

For a simpler method,
and a milder flavor,
omit the oil and cook
the squash, pears,
rosemary and water in
a medium saucepan
over medium heat
until very tender, about
20 minutes. Purée on
high speed as in Step 3.

Roasted Squash and Pears

Preheat oven to 400°F (200°C)
Rimmed baking sheet, lined with foil

1 ½ cups	cubed peeled butternut squash	375 mL
1 cup	cubed peeled pear (about 1)	250 mL
1 tbsp	olive oil	15 mL
1 tsp	crumbled dried rosemary (optional)	5 mL
½ cup	water (approx.)	125 mL

1. In a medium bowl, toss squash and pear with oil and rosemary, if using.

2. Arrange in a single layer on prepared baking sheet and roast in preheated oven until squash and pears are golden and tender, about 20 minutes. Let cool.

3. Transfer to blender, add water and purée on high speed, adding more water if necessary, until smooth.

**Nutritional Information
(Per ¼-cup/60 mL Serving)**

Calories	39 Kcal
Total Carbohydrates	6 g
Fiber	1 g
Fat	2 g
Protein	0 g
Iron	0 mg

Squash and Split Peas

1 cup	cubed peeled squash	250 mL
½ cup	split peas, rinsed	125 mL
1 cup	water or homemade vegetable stock	250 mL

Adding split peas to a favorite vegetable like squash adds extra fiber and protein.

1. In a small saucepan, combine squash, peas and water. Bring to a simmer over medium heat. Cover and cook about 15 minutes or until peas and squash are tender. Let cool slightly.

2. Transfer to blender and purée on high speed until smooth.

**Nutritional Information
(Per ¼-cup/60 mL Serving)**

Calories	51 Kcal
Total Carbohydrates	10 g
Fiber	0.3 g
Fat	0 g
Protein	3 g
Iron	0.6 mg

**MAKES ABOUT
2 CUPS (500 ML)**

*Pairing broccoli with
the mild, sweet flavors
of squash and carrots
is a great way to
introduce it.*

TIPS

Cut the vegetables into
equal-sized pieces for
even cooking.

Cook vegetables until
they break apart when
pierced with a fork;
this will ensure the
smoothest consistency
when the vegetables
are puréed.

Squashed Vegetable Purée

1 cup	diced peeled butternut squash	250 mL
½ cup	sliced peeled broccoli stems	125 mL
½ cup	diced peeled carrot (about 1)	125 mL
¼ cup	orange juice	60 mL

1. Place squash, broccoli stems and carrot in a steaming basket fitted over a saucepan of boiling water. Cover and steam for 15 to 20 minutes, or until very tender. Let cool.

2. Transfer vegetables to blender, add orange juice and purée on high speed until smooth.

**Nutritional Information
(Per ¼-cup/60 mL Serving)**

Calories . . . . 16 Kcal
Total Carbohydrates . . . . 4 g
Fiber . . . . 1 g
Fat . . . . 0 g
Protein . . . . 0 g
Iron . . . . 0 mg

Squash, Celery Root and Apples

1 cup	diced peeled acorn squash	250 mL
1 cup	diced peeled apple (about 1)	250 mL
½ cup	diced peeled celery root	125 mL
½ cup	unsweetened apple juice	125 mL
¼ tsp	ground nutmeg	1 mL

1. In a medium saucepan, over medium-low heat, combine squash, apple, celery root, apple juice and nutmeg. Bring to a simmer, cover and cook, stirring occasionally, until squash, celery root and apples are very tender, about 35 minutes. Let cool.

2. Transfer to blender and purée on high speed until smooth.

**MAKES ABOUT
2 CUPS (500 ML)**

Celeriac, or celery root, is the root of a specific variety of celery. Peel the tough outer skin before dicing the flesh inside.

VARIATION

Substitute an equal amount of chopped celery for the celery root.

**Nutritional Information
(Per ¼-cup/60 mL Serving)**

Calories	24 Kcal
Total Carbohydrates	6 g
Fiber	1 g
Fat	0 g
Protein	0 g
Iron	0 mg

Baking the apples and squash maximizes their flavor and brings their natural sugars to life.

FOR OLDER KIDS

Put ½ cup (125 mL) squashed apples in a ramekin. Toss ¼ cup (60 mL) granola cereal with 1 tbsp (15 mL) melted butter and sprinkle over top. Bake in oven preheated to 350°F (180°C) until granola is golden, about 12 minutes.

VARIATION

Omit oil and syrup and combine apples, squash, nutmeg and apple juice in a medium saucepan over medium heat. Bring to a simmer, cover and cook until very tender, about 20 minutes; purée on high speed in blender until smooth.

Squashed Apples

Preheat oven to 350°F (180°C)
Rimmed baking sheet, lined with foil

2 cups	diced peeled butternut squash	500 mL
1 cup	diced peeled Golden Delicious apple (about 1)	250 mL
1 tbsp	vegetable oil	15 mL
1 tsp	pure maple syrup	5 mL
Pinch	ground nutmeg	Pinch
½ cup	unsweetened apple juice or water	125 mL

1. In a medium bowl, toss squash and apple with oil, maple syrup and nutmeg.

2. Spread on prepared baking sheet and bake in preheated oven until apples and squash are tender and golden, about 30 minutes. Let cool.

3. In blender, combine apple mixture and apple juice and purée on high speed until smooth.

Nutritional Information (Per ¼-cup/60 mL Serving)	
Calories	46 Kcal
Total Carbohydrates	8 g
Fiber	1 g
Fat	2 g
Protein	0 g
Iron	0 mg

Squashed Green Beans

1 cup	diced peeled butternut squash	250 mL
½ cup	unsweetened apple juice or water	125 mL
1½ cups	sliced trimmed green beans (about 6 oz/175 g)	375 mL

Taste the fall harvest in this rich vegetable purée!

1. In a medium saucepan, over medium-high heat, combine squash and apple juice. Add enough water to completely cover squash. Cover and bring to a boil; reduce heat and simmer for 10 minutes. Add green beans, cover and cook until beans and squash are very tender, about 10 minutes. Let cool.

2. Transfer to blender with cooking liquid and purée on high speed until smooth.

**Nutritional Information
(Per ¼-cup/60 mL Serving)**

Calories	43 Kcal
Total Carbohydrates	11 g
Fiber	2 g
Fat	0 g
Protein	1 g
Iron	1 mg

*Leeks have a delicate,
subtle flavor that is
much sweeter and
milder than cooking
onions. They're a great
way to get your little
one started.*

VARIATION

Whisk ½ cup (125 mL)
cold milk into 1 cup
(250 mL) purée for a
refreshing summer soup.

Summer Savory

1 tbsp	vegetable oil	15 mL
½ cup	sliced leeks, white and light green parts only	125 mL
1 cup	diced peeled potatoes (about 1 large)	250 mL
½ cup	frozen corn kernels	125 mL
½ cup	diced tomatoes	125 mL
½ cup	water or homemade vegetable stock (see page 62)	125 mL
1 tbsp	chopped fresh parsley	15 mL

1. In a medium saucepan, heat oil over medium-high heat. Add leeks and cook, stirring, until tender, but not browned, about 5 minutes.

2. Add potatoes, corn and tomatoes and cook, stirring, until potatoes are golden, about 5 minutes.

3. Add water and reduce heat to medium. Cover and simmer until potatoes are tender, about 15 minutes. Stir in parsley. Let cool.

4. Transfer to blender with cooking liquid and purée on high speed until desired consistency is reached.

**Nutritional Information
(Per ¼-cup/60 mL Serving)**

Calories	47 Kcal
Total Carbohydrates	7 g
Fiber	1 g
Fat	2 g
Protein	2 g
Iron	0 mg

Sweet Potato Hummus

½ cup	cooked peeled sweet potato	125 mL
½ cup	canned chickpeas, rinsed and drained	125 mL
½ cup	water	125 mL

Vitamin C from the sweet potato will help baby absorb iron in the chickpeas.

1. Place sweet potato, chickpeas and water in blender. Purée on high speed until smooth.

2. *Make ahead:* Store in an airtight container in the refrigerator for up to 3 days. Do not freeze.

**Nutritional Information
(Per ¼-cup/60 mL Serving)**

Calories	75 Kcal
Total Carbohydrates	14 g
Fiber	2 g
Fat	0.4 g
Protein	2 g
Iron	0.4 mg
Vitamin C	8 mg

6

*In general, the darker
the color of vegetable,
the stronger the taste.
If you don't succeed
with broccoli on its
own, try combining it
with any of your baby's
favorites until they
become used to it.*

Yummy Broccoli

| 3 cups | broccoli florets | 750 mL |
| 1/2 cup | unsweetened apple juice or water | 125 mL |

1. Place broccoli in a steaming basket fitted over a
saucepan of boiling water. Cover and steam until
broccoli is very tender, about 15 to 20 minutes.
Let cool.

2. Transfer broccoli to blender, add apple juice and
purée on high speed until smooth.

**Nutritional Information
(Per 1/4-cup/60 mL Serving)**

Calories . . . . 22 Kcal
Total Carbohydrates . . . . 5 g
Fiber . . . . 1 g
Fat . . . . 0 g
Protein . . . . 1 g
Iron . . . . 0 mg
Vitamin C . . . . 25 mg

Avocado, Mango and Lime

½ cup	diced peeled avocado (about ½)	125 mL
½ cup	diced peeled mango (about ½)	125 mL
2 tbsp	freshly squeezed lime juice	30 mL

1. In blender, combine avocado, mango and lime juice and purée on high speed until smooth.

2. *Make ahead:* Store in an airtight container in the refrigerator for up to 1 day.

**Nutritional Information
(Per ¼-cup/60 mL Serving)**

Calories	44 Kcal
Total Carbohydrates	5 g
Fiber	1 g
Fat	3 g
Protein	0 g
Iron	0 mg

**MAKES ABOUT
1 CUP (500 ML)**

TIPS

Avocados offer more protein than any other fruit and are high in essential fatty acids, ideal for baby's development.

Prevent discoloration of the avocado's flesh by sprinkling it with lemon or lime juice.

Summer fruits are combined in this quick and easy dessert.

TIP

Buy pitted cherries during the summer and keep them portioned in your freezer for easy use throughout the year.

FOR OLDER KIDS

Freeze mixture in ice-pop molds for a chilly treat.

Cherried Peaches

2 cups	sliced peeled peaches (about 3)	500 mL
1 cup	pitted red sour cherries (about 8 oz/250 g)	250 mL
½ cup	peach nectar	125 mL

1. In blender, combine peaches, cherries and peach nectar and purée on high speed until smooth.

**Nutritional Information
(Per ¼-cup/60 mL Serving)**

Calories . . . . 36 Kcal
Total Carbohydrates . . . . 9 g
Fiber . . . . 1 g
Fat . . . . 0 g
Protein . . . . 1 g
Iron . . . . 0 mg

Cranberry Apple Mush

4 cups	sliced peeled apples (about 3 large)	1 L
½ cup	fresh or frozen cranberries	125 mL
½ cup	sweetened apple juice	125 mL
1 tsp	ground cinnamon	5 mL

1. In a medium saucepan, over medium-high heat, bring apples, cranberries, apple juice and cinnamon to a boil. Cover, reduce heat and simmer until apples are very tender, about 25 minutes. Let cool.

2. Transfer to blender and purée on high speed until smooth.

Nutritional Information
(Per ¼-cup/60 mL Serving)

Calories	44 Kcal
Total Carbohydrates	11 g
Fiber	2 g
Fat	0 g
Protein	0 g
Iron	0 mg

MAKES ABOUT 2 CUPS (500 ML)

Everyday apples get some zip from tart autumn cranberries.

TIP

Cranberries are known to be effective in preventing urinary tract infections.

**MAKES ABOUT
2 CUPS (500 ML)**

*Figs are a good source
of potassium and fiber;
paired with the mild,
sweet taste of pears
(which are also a good
source of soluble fiber),
this purée is a great
spread for adults too!*

Figgy Pears

1 1/2 cups	diced peeled pears (about 2)	375 mL
3/4 cup	unsweetened orange juice	175 mL
1/2 cup	diced figs, stems removed (about 4 oz/125 g)	125 mL
1/4 tsp	ground allspice	1 mL

1. In a medium saucepan, over medium-low heat, combine pears, orange juice, figs and allspice. Bring to a simmer, cover and cook until pears and figs are very tender, about 20 minutes. Let cool.

2. Transfer to blender and purée on high speed until smooth.

**Nutritional Information
(Per 1/4-cup/60 mL Serving)**

Calories . . . . 44 Kcal
Total Carbohydrates . . . . .11 g
Fiber. . . . . .1 g
Fat. . . . . .0 g
Protein . . . . .0 g
Iron. . . . . 0 mg

Guacamole
for Beginners

1 cup	sliced peeled avocado (about 1)	250 mL
1/2 cup	chopped peeled and seeded tomato	125 mL
2 tbsp	freshly squeezed lime juice	30 mL

1. In blender, combine avocado, tomato and lime juice and purée on high speed until smooth.

2. *Make ahead:* Store in an airtight container in the refrigerator for up to 3 days. Do not freeze.

Nutritional Information
(Per 1/4-cup/60 mL Serving)

Calories	65 Kcal
Total Carbohydrates	4 g
Fiber	1 g
Fat	6 g
Protein	1 g
Iron	0 mg

**MAKES ABOUT
1 CUP (250 ML)**

FOR OLDER KIDS

Serve as a dip with baked whole wheat tortilla or pita wedges.

*Blended melon flavors
combine in a refreshing
treat for your baby.*

TIPS

To peel melons: Cut
in half and reserve
one half for later use.
Cut the other half
lengthwise into four
wedges. Peel the wedges
and discard seeds, if
any.

Choose melons that
are unblemished,
fragrant and heavy
for their size.

FOR OLDER KIDS

Freeze unused chopped
peeled melon in an
airtight container in
the freezer. In blender,
combine 1 cup (250 mL)
frozen melon pieces
and purée on high
speed until smooth
for an icy treat.

Melon Madness

1 cup	diced cantaloupe	250 mL
1 cup	diced honeydew melon	250 mL
1 cup	diced seedless watermelon	250 mL

1. In blender, combine cantaloupe, honeydew and
watermelon and purée on high speed until smooth.

**Nutritional Information
(Per $\frac{1}{4}$-cup/60 mL Serving)**

Calories	21 Kcal
Total Carbohydrates	5 g
Fiber	0 g
Fat	0 g
Protein	0 g
Iron	0 mg

Orange, Orange, Orange

1 cup	diced peeled carrots (about 2)	250 mL
1 cup	diced peeled sweet potato (about 1/2)	250 mL
1/2 cup	diced peeled pear (about 1/2)	125 mL
1/2 cup	orange juice (see tip, at right)	125 mL
1/2 cup	water	125 mL

1. In a medium saucepan, over medium-high heat, bring carrots, sweet potato, pear, orange juice and water to a boil. Cover, reduce heat and simmer until vegetables are very tender, about 20 minutes. Let cool.

2. Transfer to blender with cooking liquid and purée on high speed, adding more water if necessary, until smooth.

**Nutritional Information
(Per 1/4-cup/60 mL Serving)**

Calories	71 Kcal
Total Carbohydrates	12 g
Fiber	1 g
Fat	2 g
Protein	1 g
Iron	0 mg

**MAKES ABOUT
2 CUPS (500 ML)**

A deep orange color is generally an indication that the fruit or vegetable contains beta carotene and vitamin C — this purée is a triple dose, packed with flavor!

TIP

Substitute additional water for the orange juice for young stomachs that are irritated by citrus.

FOR OLDER KIDS

Add a dash of curry powder and 2 cups (500 mL) homemade vegetable or chicken stock (see page 62) while cooking to make a delicious soup. Serve with warm whole-grain rolls.

FOR OLDER KIDS

For a special treat, stir this purée into their favorite porridge with a sprinkle of ground cinnamon.

Peach-Pear Bananarama

1 ½ cups	diced peeled peaches (about 2)	375 mL
1 cup	diced peeled pear (about 1)	250 mL
1	banana, sliced	1

1. In blender, combine peaches, pear and banana and purée on high speed until smooth.

> **Nutritional Information**
> **(Per ¼-cup/60 mL Serving)**
>
> Calories . . . . 29 Kcal
> Total Carbohydrates . . . . 7 g
> Fiber . . . . 1 g
> Fat . . . . 0 g
> Protein . . . . 0 g
> Iron . . . . 0 mg

Rhubarb, Apples and Berries

2 cups	sliced peeled apples (about 2)	500 mL
1 cup	chopped rhubarb (about 2 stalks)	250 mL
¼ cup	raspberries and/or blueberries	60 mL
¼ cup	frozen apple juice concentrate	60 mL

1. In a medium saucepan, over medium-low heat, combine apples, rhubarb, berries and apple juice concentrate. Bring to a simmer, cover and cook, stirring occasionally, until fruit is very tender, about 30 minutes. Let cool.

2. Transfer to blender and purée on high speed until smooth.

**Nutritional Information
(Per ¼-cup/60 mL Serving)**

Calories	36 Kcal
Total Carbohydrates	9 g
Fiber	1 g
Fat	0 g
Protein	0 g
Iron	0 mg

**MAKES ABOUT
2 CUPS (500 ML)**

TIP

Use an equal amount of frozen berries when fresh are not in season.

Creamy apricots make this strawberry purée an absolute delight!

TIPS

Apricots are an excellent source of vitamin A. When fresh are not in season, used dried that have been rehydrated in boiling water for 30 minutes, or until swollen and softened. Use liquid with apricots.

Serve this over angel food cake topped with vanilla ice cream… yum! Who said baby food wasn't for everyone?

Strawberry Decadence

1 cup	fresh or frozen strawberries	250 mL
1 cup	sliced apricots (2 to 3)	250 mL
	Zest and juice of 1 lemon	

1. In blender, combine strawberries, apricots, and lemon zest and juice and purée on high speed until smooth.

2. *Make ahead:* Store in an airtight container in the refrigerator for up to 1 week.

Nutritional Information (Per ¼-cup/60 mL Serving)	
Calories	17 Kcal
Total Carbohydrates	4 g
Fiber	1 g
Fat	0 g
Protein	0 g
Iron	0 mg

Tropical Fruit Breeze

1 cup	chopped peeled kiwi (about 2)	250 mL
½ cup	sliced banana (about 1 small)	125 mL
½ cup	chopped peeled mango (about ½)	125 mL
½ cup	orange juice	125 mL

1. In blender, combine kiwi, banana, mango and orange juice and purée on high speed until smooth.

2. *Make ahead:* Store in an airtight container in the refrigerator for up to 5 days.

**Nutritional Information
(Per ½-cup/125 mL Serving)**

Calories	107 Kcal
Total Carbohydrates	27 g
Fiber	3 g
Fat	1 g
Protein	1 g
Iron	0 mg
Vitamin C	54 mg

**MAKES ABOUT
2 CUPS (500 ML)**

FOR OLDER KIDS

To make a great smoothie, add ½ cup (125 mL) milk to 1 cup (250 mL) of the purée.

*Watermelon blends
well with other fruits
to make a naturally
sweet thirst quencher.*

TIP

Use an equal amount
of frozen strawberries
when fresh are not
in season.

FOR OLDER KIDS

Freeze purée in ice-pop
molds for a frosty treat.

Watermelon Refresher

2 cups	diced seedless watermelon	500 mL
1/2 cup	diced peeled kiwi (about 1)	125 mL
1/2 cup	sliced strawberries	125 mL
1 tbsp	lime juice	15 mL

1. In blender, combine watermelon, kiwi, strawberries
and lime juice and purée on high speed until smooth.

**Nutritional Information
(Per 1/4-cup/60 mL Serving)**

Calories . . . . 22 Kcal
Total Carbohydrates . . . . 5 g
Fiber . . . . 1 g
Fat . . . . 0 g
Protein . . . . 0 g
Iron . . . . 0 mg

Squash and Pepper Risotto (page 124)

Vegetable Paella (page 125)

Cheesy Salmon and Broccoli Dinner (page 129)

Chili for Beginners (page 148)

Beef, Potato and Green Peas

MAKES 2 CUPS (500 ML)

This simple "stew" provides a perfect balance of flavor.

6 oz	lean ground sirloin beef	175 g
½ cup	potatoes, peeled and diced	125 mL
1 cup	water or homemade beef stock (see page 63)	250 mL
½ cup	frozen peas	125 mL

1. In a non-stick skillet, brown beef with potatoes. Drain off fat. Add water and simmer until potatoes are tender, about 15 minutes. Add peas and cook one minute. Let cool.

2. Transfer to blender and purée on high speed to desired consistency.

Nutritional Information
(Per ¼-cup/60 mL Serving)

Calories	50 Kcal
Total Carbohydrates	3 g
Fiber	0.6 g
Fat	2 g
Protein	5 g
Iron	0.4 mg

*Classic comfort food
for your baby!*

FOR OLDER KIDS

Put ½ cup (125 mL)
purée in a ramekin
or gratin dish. Use
refrigerated dinner-roll
dough (cut to fit) to
cover, using excess to
form your child's initial
and place on top. Bake
in preheated 350°F
(180°C) oven until
pastry is golden and
filling is warm, about
12 minutes.

Chicken Stew

1 tbsp	vegetable oil	15 mL
6 oz	boneless skinless chicken breast, chopped	175 g
½ cup	diced peeled carrot	125 mL
¼ cup	diced onion	60 mL
¼ cup	diced celery	60 mL
1	small potato, cubed	1
1 cup	water or homemade chicken stock	250 mL
1 tbsp	minced fresh parsley	15 mL

1. In a medium saucepan, heat oil over medium-high heat. Add chicken, turning to brown evenly; transfer to a plate.

2. Add carrot, onion and celery to saucepan; cook until tender but not browned, about 5 minutes. Stir in potato and water; bring to a boil. Return browned chicken to pan. Cover, reduce heat and simmer until potatoes are very tender and chicken is no longer pink inside, about 20 minutes. Stir in parsley. Let cool.

3. Transfer to blender and purée on high speed to desired consistency.

**Nutritional Information
(Per ½-cup/125 mL Serving)**

Calories . . . . 120 Kcal
Total Carbohydrates . . . . 7 g
Fiber . . . . 1 g
Fat . . . . 4 g
Protein . . . . 14 g
Iron . . . . 1 mg

Chicken with Celery

6 oz	boneless skinless chicken breast, diced	175 g
1 cup	chopped celery	250 mL
1 cup	water or homemade chicken stock	250 mL

1. In a medium saucepan, combine chicken, celery and water; bring to a simmer over medium heat. Cover and simmer until celery is very tender and chicken is no longer pink inside, about 15 minutes. Let cool.

2. Transfer to blender and purée on high speed until smooth.

Nutritional Information
(Per ½-cup/125 mL Serving)

Calories . . . . 42 Kcal
Total Carbohydrates . . . . 2 g
Fiber . . . . 1 g
Fat . . . . 0 g
Protein . . . . 8 g
Iron . . . . 1 mg

**MAKES ABOUT
2 CUPS (500 ML)**

Kids love the mild flavors of chicken and celery.

TIP

For a smooth purée, remove the tough fibers from the celery ribs before chopping.

FOR OLDER KIDS

Stir purée into cooked brown rice for a quick meal.

6

FOR OLDER KIDS

Serve as a dip for
vegetables and strips
of baked whole-wheat
pitas.

Hummus for Beginners

| 1 cup | rinsed and drained canned chickpeas | 250 mL |
| ½ cup | water | 125 mL |

1. In blender, on high speed, purée chickpeas until smooth.

2. *Make ahead:* Store in an airtight container in the refrigerator for up to 3 days. Do not freeze.

**Nutritional Information
(Per ¼-cup/60 mL Serving)**

Calories . . . . 71 Kcal
Total Carbohydrates . . . . 14 g
Fiber . . . . 3 g
Fat . . . . 1 g
Protein . . . . 3 g
Iron . . . . 1 mg

Turkey and Apricots

1 cup	dried apricots	250 mL
1 1/2 cups	water	375 mL
6 oz	boneless skinless turkey, diced	175 g

1. In a medium saucepan, combine apricots and water over medium-high heat and simmer for 10 minutes. Add turkey; continue simmering until turkey is cooked through, about 10 minutes. Let cool.

2. Transfer to blender and purée on high speed to desired consistency.

Nutritional Information (Per 1/4-cup/60 mL Serving)

Calories	45 Kcal
Total Carbohydrates	5 g
Fiber	0.4 g
Fat	0 g
Protein	5 g
Iron	0.6 mg

MAKES 2 CUPS (500 ML)

Apricots are a great source of fiber and vitamin A, and they go really well with poultry.

Pairing meat with fruit brings out great flavor and is a simple way for little ones to get their protein.

Pork and Peaches

6 oz	pork tenderloin, diced	175 g
1 cup	fresh or frozen peaches	250 mL
½ cup	water	125 mL

1. In a small saucepan, combine pork, peaches and water. Cook over medium high heat until pork is no longer pink, about 10 minutes. Let cool.

2. Transfer to blender and purée on high speed to desired consistency.

Nutritional Information (Per ¼-cup/60 mL Serving)	
Calories	54 Kcal
Total Carbohydrates	1 g
Fiber	0.3 g
Fat	2 g
Protein	7 g
Iron	0.2 mg

FOOD FOR BABIES

Eight Months and Older

Continued on next page

Meal Plans

At this age, babies are ready to try using a cup. Breast milk, formula and water are good choices to offer in a regular cup or a "sippy" cup. Babies can also begin to discover the wide array of grain products. Continue breastfeeding or formula feeding on demand throughout the day. See the introduction for more information on these meal plans. Please note that the amounts are just suggestions. All babies are different and require different amounts of food. Let your baby eat until he or she turns away or appears full.

MEAL Plan for babies 8 months and older

MEAL	1	2	3
Breakfast	• 2 tbsp (30 mL) prepared iron-fortified infant cereal • ¼ cup (60 mL) Peach-Pear Bananarama (page 92)	• ¼ cup (60 mL) Peach and Banana Oatmeal (page 121) • ¼ cup (60 mL) Pears (page 52)	• 2 tbsp (30 mL) prepared iron-fortified infant cereal • ¼ cup (60 mL) Apricots (page 44)
Snack	• Breast or formula feeding on demand	• Breast or formula feeding on demand	• Breast or formula feeding on demand
Lunch	• ¼ cup (60 mL) Sweet Potatoes (page 40) • ¼ cup (60 mL) Chicken (page 58)	• ¼ cup (60 mL) Chicken with Pumpkin (page 140)	• ¼ cup (60 mL) Chicken Quinoa Stew (page 138)
Snack	• Breast or formula feeding on demand	• Breast or formula feeding on demand	• Breast or formula feeding on demand
Supper	• ¼ cup (60 mL) Lentil and Rice Pilaf (page 120) • ¼ cup (60 mL) Apples (page 43)	• ¼ cup (60 mL) Chicken Jambalaya (page 136) • ¼ cup (60 mL) Squashed Green Beans (page 81)	• ¼ cup (60 mL) Spaghetti Bolognese (page 146)
Snack	• Breast or formula feeding on demand	• Breast or formula feeding on demand	• Breast or formula feeding on demand

This complete meal is nutritious and has a sweet, mellow flavor that babies love.

Butternut Squash, Corn and Tofu

1 cup	diced peeled butternut squash	250 mL
1 cup	water or homemade vegetable stock (see page 62)	250 mL
½ cup	frozen corn	125 mL
¼ cup	silken tofu (about 2 oz/60 g)	60 mL

1. In a medium saucepan, bring squash and water to a boil over medium-high heat. Cover, reduce heat and simmer until squash is tender, about 20 minutes. Stir in corn and cook for 5 minutes more. Let cool.

2. Transfer to blender, add tofu and purée on high speed until smooth.

Nutritional Information
(Per ½-cup/125 mL Serving)

Calories . . . . .58 Kcal
Total Carbohydrates . . . . .9 g
Fiber . . . . .2 g
Fat . . . . .1 g
Protein . . . . .5 g
Iron . . . . .2 mg

Summer Succotash

1 tbsp	vegetable oil	15 mL
½ cup	chopped onion	125 mL
1 cup	frozen corn	250 mL
1 cup	frozen lima beans	250 mL
1 cup	diced tomatoes	250 mL
½ cup	water or homemade vegetable stock (see page 62)	125 mL
1 tbsp	chopped fresh parsley	15 mL

Don't assume your child will have the same food dislikes you do. Most food preferences are learned. Lima beans offer a smooth, buttery texture that appeals to babies.

1. In a skillet, heat oil over medium-high heat. Add onion and cook until tender but not browned, about 5 minutes. Add corn, lima beans, tomatoes, water and parsley; bring to a boil. Cover, reduce heat and simmer, stirring occasionally, until lima beans are tender, about 15 minutes. Let cool.

2. Transfer to blender and purée on high speed until smooth.

Nutritional Information (Per ¼-cup/60 mL Serving)	
Calories	72 Kcal
Total Carbohydrates	11 g
Fiber	2 g
Fat	2 g
Protein	3 g
Iron	1 mg

**MAKES ABOUT
2 CUPS (500 ML)**

Adding tofu to fruit makes a simple complete meal without any fuss.

FOR OLDER KIDS

This recipe, or any recipe that combines silken tofu and puréed fruits, can help toddlers who avoid meat get some protein.

Apples, Plums and Tofu

2	plums, peeled and pitted	2
1 cup	unsweetened applesauce	250 mL
¼ cup	silken tofu (about 2 oz/60 g)	60 mL

1. Combine plums, applesauce and tofu in blender and purée on high speed until smooth.

**Nutritional Information
(Per ½-cup/125 mL Serving)**

Calories	55 Kcal
Total Carbohydrates	11 g
Fiber	1 g
Fat	1 g
Protein	2 g
Iron	1 mg

Apricots, Pears and Tofu

4	ripe apricots, pits removed	4
1	ripe pear, peeled and sliced	1
¼ cup	silken tofu (about 2 oz/60 g)	60 mL

1. Combine apricots, pear and tofu in blender and purée on high speed until smooth.

**Nutritional Information
(Per ½-cup/125 mL Serving)**

Calories . . . . 39 Kcal
Total Carbohydrates . . . . 7 g
Fiber . . . . 1 g
Fat . . . . 1 g
Protein . . . . 2 g
Iron . . . . 1 mg

**MAKES ABOUT
2 CUPS (500 ML)**

Adding tofu to any of the vegetable or fruit recipes in previous sections will offer your baby protein without the fuss of cooking meat.

TIP

"Silken" refers to the texture of the tofu; it has a greater amount of liquid.

Millet cooks fairly quickly, producing a dish that is similar to couscous but has its own distinct flavor.

Apricots with Ancient Grains

2 cups	water	500 mL
½ cup	millet	125 mL
1 cup	sliced fresh apricots	250 mL

1. In a small saucepan, over medium-high heat, bring water and millet just to a boil. Cover, reduce heat to low and simmer gently until millet is tender, about 30 minutes. Let stand, covered, until cooled slightly, about 15 minutes.

2. Transfer to blender, add apricots and purée on high speed until smooth.

**Nutritional Information
(Per ¼-cup/60 mL Serving)**

Calories . . . . 56 Kcal
Total Carbohydrates . . . . 11 g
Fiber . . . . 1 g
Fat . . . . 1 g
Protein . . . . 2 g
Iron . . . . Trace

Barley, Lentils and Sweet Potato

2 tsp	olive oil	10 mL
1	carrot, peeled and diced	1
1	stalk celery, diced	1
½	onion, diced	½
2 cups	homemade chicken stock (see page 62) or water	500 mL
½ cup	pearl barley, rinsed	125 mL
1 cup	diced peeled sweet potato	250 mL
¼ cup	dried green lentils, rinsed	60 mL

MAKES ABOUT 3 CUPS (750 ML)

TIP

Add more homemade chicken stock to this purée to make a great soup for the whole family.

1. In a medium saucepan, heat oil over medium-high heat. Add carrot, celery and onion and cook, stirring occasionally, until carrots are tender, about 5 minutes.

2. Add stock and barley and bring to a boil. Cover, reduce heat and simmer for 20 minutes. Add sweet potato and lentils. Simmer until barley, lentils and sweet potato are very tender, about 25 minutes. Let cool.

3. Transfer to blender and purée on high speed until smooth.

**Nutritional Information
(Per ½-cup/125 mL Serving)**

Calories . . . . 148 Kcal
Total Carbohydrates . . . . 26 g
Fiber . . . . 6 g
Fat . . . . 2 g
Protein . . . . 8 g
Iron . . . . 2 mg

Nutty quinoa and nutrient-dense broccoli combine in this yummy meal that is sure to be a hit.

Broccoli and Quinoa

1 ½ cups	water	375 mL
½ cup	quinoa	125 mL
1 cup	chopped broccoli	250 mL

1. In a small saucepan, bring water to a boil over medium-high heat. Add quinoa and bring back to a boil. Reduce heat to medium, cover and simmer, stirring occasionally, for 10 minutes.

2. Add broccoli and simmer 5 more minutes. Remove from heat and let sit, covered, until broccoli and quinoa are tender, about 10 minutes.

3. Transfer to blender and purée on high speed until smooth.

**Nutritional Information
(Per ¼-cup/60 mL Serving)**

Calories . . . . 42 Kcal
Total Carbohydrates . . . . 8 g
Fiber . . . . 1 g
Fat. . . . . 0.7 g
Protein . . . . 2 g
Iron. . . . . 1 mg

Brown Rice and Tomatoes with Cabbage

1 tbsp	vegetable oil	15 mL
1/2 cup	chopped onion	125 mL
1 cup	shredded cabbage	250 mL
1 1/4 cup	canned diced tomatoes, with juice	300 mL
1/2 cup	brown rice	125 mL
1/2 cup	water	125 mL

1. In a medium saucepan, heat oil over medium-high heat. Add onion and cook, stirring, until tender, about 3 minutes. Add cabbage and cook, stirring occasionally, until softened, about 5 minutes.

2. Add tomatoes with juice, rice and water; bring to a boil. Cover, reduce heat and simmer until rice is tender and most of the liquid has been absorbed, about 40 minutes. Remove from heat and let stand, covered, for 5 minutes.

3. Transfer to blender and purée on high speed to desired consistency.

Nutritional Information
(Per 1/4-cup/60 mL Serving)

Calories	71 Kcal
Total Carbohydrates	12 g
Fiber	1 g
Fat	2 g
Protein	1 g
Iron	0 mg

MAKES ABOUT 2 CUPS (500 ML)

Babies like cabbage's mild flavor, and it stimulates the appetite and has antidiarrheal and antibiotic properties. It also stimulates flatulence, so feed it to your baby in moderation.

TIP

If your baby is over eight months, serve with puréed pork or beef for a full meal.

VARIATION

Once your baby is used to cabbage, try the Savoy variety, which offers more flavor.

**MAKES ABOUT
2 CUPS (500 ML)**

Couscous refers to tiny beads of semolina that have been mixed with cold salted water. It is eaten much like rice or other cereal grains. This recipe calls for the whole-wheat variety, which has a slightly nutty flavor.

Citrus Couscous

½ cup	orange juice	125 mL
1 cup	water or homemade chicken stock (see page 62)	250 mL
1 cup	whole wheat couscous	250 mL
1 tbsp	olive oil	15 mL
¼ cup	chopped onion	60 mL
½ cup	chopped oranges	125 mL
1 tbsp	chopped parsley	15 mL

1. In a medium saucepan, bring orange juice and water to a boil. Add couscous; cover and remove from heat. Let sit for 5 minutes or until most of the liquid is absorbed and couscous is tender. Let cool.

2. Meanwhile, in a skillet, heat oil over medium-high heat. Add onion and cook, stirring, until tender, about 5 minutes.

3. Transfer onions and couscous to blender. Add oranges and purée on high speed to desired consistency. Sprinkle with parsley.

Nutritional Information **(Per ¼-cup/60 mL Serving)**
Calories . . . . 117 Kcal
Total Carbohydrates . . . . 20 g
Fiber . . . . 1 g
Fat . . . . 2 g
Protein . . . . 4 g
Iron . . . . Trace

Dhal for Beginners

1 1/2 cups	water or homemade vegetable stock (see page 62)	375 mL
1/4 cup	dried red lentils, rinsed	60 mL
1/2 tsp	ground coriander	2 mL
1/4 tsp	ground turmeric	1 mL
1	small potato, peeled and diced	1
1	carrot, peeled and diced	1
1/2 cup	cauliflower florets	125 mL

MAKES ABOUT 2 CUPS (500 ML)

This intensely colored purée is packed full of delicious nutrients.

FOR OLDER KIDS

Serve as a dip with warm naan bread or whole wheat pita wedges.

1. In a medium saucepan, combine water, lentils, coriander and turmeric; bring to a boil. Cover, reduce heat and simmer for 15 minutes, until lentils are slightly tender.

2. Stir in potato, carrot and cauliflower; cover and simmer until vegetables and lentils are very tender, about 15 minutes. Let cool.

3. Transfer to blender and purée on high speed until smooth.

Nutritional Information
(Per 1/4-cup/60 mL Serving)

Calories	84 Kcal
Total Carbohydrates	13 g
Fiber	6 g
Fat	0 g
Protein	8 g
Iron	2 mg

*Try this as a great
substitute for classic
oatmeal.*

Fruity Quinoa Breakfast Cereal

2 cups	water or rice beverage	500 mL
½ cup	quinoa	125 mL
¼ cup	grated peeled apple	60 mL
¼ cup	chopped banana	60 mL
Pinch	cinnamon (optional)	Pinch

1. In a medium saucepan, bring water to a boil over medium-high heat. Add quinoa and bring back to a boil. Reduce heat, cover and simmer, stirring occasionally, for 10 minutes. Remove from heat and leave covered until quinoa is tender, about 10 minutes.

2. Transfer quinoa and remaining liquid to a blender. Add apple, banana and cinnamon, if using; purée on high speed until smooth.

**Nutritional Information
(Per ¼-cup/60 mL Serving)**

Calories	56 Kcal
Total Carbohydrates	10 g
Fiber	3 g
Fat	1 g
Protein	2 g
Iron	0.6 mg

Green Rice

**MAKES ABOUT
2 CUPS (500 ML)**

2 tbsp	olive oil	30 mL
1/4 cup	sliced onion	60 mL
1	clove garlic, minced	1
4 cups	leafy greens (spinach, Swiss chard or kale)	1 L
1/4 tsp	salt	1 mL
1/4 tsp	grated lemon zest	2 mL
1 cup	cooked rice, any variety	250 mL

FOR OLDER KIDS

For more flavor, purée 1/4 cup (60 mL) toasted pine nuts with the greens.

1. In a skillet, heat oil over medium-high heat. Add onion and cook, stirring occasionally, until tender, about 5 minutes. Add garlic and cook for 1 minute. Stir in greens until wilted, about 1 minute. Sprinkle with salt and lemon zest. Let cool slightly.

2. Transfer to blender and purée on high speed until smooth. Stir in rice until rice is coated with greens.

**Nutritional Information
(Per 1/4-cup/60 mL Serving)**

Calories	65 Kcal
Total Carbohydrates	7 g
Fiber	1 g
Fat	3 g
Protein	1 g
Iron	Trace

**MAKES ABOUT
2 CUPS (500 ML)**

*Rice cooked in stock
with vegetables and
spice provides energy
for the day!*

TIP

For a flavor boost, add
a pinch of chili powder
to the carrot mixture.

Jumpin' Jambalaya

1 tbsp	olive oil	15 mL
1/2 cup	chopped peeled carrot	125 mL
1/4 cup	chopped onion	60 mL
1/4 cup	chopped celery	60 mL
1/4 cup	long-grain white rice	60 mL
1 cup	water or homemade chicken stock (see page 62)	250 mL
1	bay leaf	1

1. In a skillet, heat oil over medium-high heat. Add carrot, onion and celery; cook, stirring, until onion is tender, about 5 minutes. Stir in rice until coated with oil. Add water and bay leaf; bring to a boil. Cover, reduce heat to low and simmer until rice is tender and most of the liquid has been absorbed, about 20 minutes. Let cool. Discard bay leaf.

2. Transfer to blender and purée on high speed to desired consistency.

**Nutritional Information
(Per 1/4-cup/60 mL Serving)**

Calories . . . . 48 Kcal
Total Carbohydrates . . . . 6 g
Fiber . . . . 0 g
Fat . . . . 2 g
Protein . . . . 2 g
Iron . . . . 0 mg

Lemon Chickpeas with Carrots and Celery

1 cup	dried chickpeas	250 mL
2 cups	water	500 mL
1 tsp	vegetable oil	5 mL
¼ cup	diced onion	60 mL
¼ cup	diced celery	60 mL
¼ cup	diced peeled carrot	60 mL
1 cup	water or homemade vegetable stock (see page 62)	250 mL
1	bay leaf	1
1 tbsp	freshly squeezed lemon juice	15 mL
1 tbsp	chopped fresh parsley	15 mL

1. In a medium bowl, soak chickpeas in water overnight or for up to 1 day. Drain and set aside.

2. In a medium saucepan, heat oil over medium-high heat. Add onion, celery and carrot and cook until tender, about 5 minutes. Add water, chickpeas and bay leaf; bring to a boil. Cover, reduce heat and simmer until chickpeas are very tender, about 45 minutes. Let cool.

3. Transfer to blender, add lemon juice and parsley and purée on high speed, adding water if necessary, until smooth.

Nutritional Information
(Per ½-cup/125 mL Serving)

Calories	139 Kcal
Total Carbohydrates	23 g
Fiber	5 g
Fat	2 g
Protein	8 g
Iron	2 mg

MAKES ABOUT 2 CUPS (500 ML)

Many of my students would like to offer beans and legumes to their babies but aren't sure what to do with them — here's a simple way to start.

TIPS

Soaking dried beans and legumes overnight decreases cooking time, preserves nutrients and reduces the flatulence they can cause.

Quick soak method: In a saucepan, combine 3 parts water with 1 part dried beans; bring to a boil over medium heat. Remove from heat and let stand, covered, for 1 to 2 hours. Drain. Cook according to recipe.

**MAKES ABOUT
2 CUPS (500 ML)**

*Lentils and rice work
well in combination
because they have
complementary amino
acids, enhancing the
nutritional value of
both foods.*

TIP

Always rinse dried
lentils well before
using — they often
contain small stones.

Lentil and Rice Pilaf

1 tbsp	olive oil	15 mL
1/2 cup	chopped onion	125 mL
1/2 cup	long-grain white rice	125 mL
1/2 tsp	curry powder	2 mL
1 cup	homemade chicken stock (see page 62)	250 mL
1 cup	water	250 mL
1/2 cup	dried red lentils, rinsed	125 mL

1. In a medium saucepan, heat oil over medium-high heat. Add onion and cook, stirring, until tender, about 5 minutes. Stir in rice and curry powder until coated with oil. Pour in chicken stock, water and lentils; bring to a boil. Cover, reduce heat to low and simmer until liquid has been absorbed and rice and lentils are tender, about 20 minutes. Let cool.

2. Transfer to blender and purée on high speed to desired consistency.

Nutritional Information (Per 1/4-cup/60 mL Serving)	
Calories	108 Kcal
Total Carbohydrates	17 g
Fiber	4 g
Fat	2 g
Protein	6 g
Iron	2 mg

Peach and Banana Oatmeal

**MAKES ABOUT
2 CUPS (500 ML)**

The carbohydrates provided by this hearty breakfast will give your little one lots of energy to get through the day.

1	banana, sliced	1
1 cup	cooked oatmeal	250 mL
1 cup	sliced, peeled peaches	250 mL

1. Place banana, oatmeal and peaches in blender; purée on high speed until smooth.

**Nutritional Information
(Per ¼-cup/60 mL Serving)**

Calories	40 Kcal
Total Carbohydrates	9 g
Fiber	1 g
Fat	0 g
Protein	1 g
Iron	1 mg

**MAKES ABOUT
2 CUPS (500 ML)**

TIP

Toss this purée with whole wheat couscous to make a nutritious vegetarian meal for the whole family.

Pumpkin and Chickpea Stew

1 cup	cubed peeled pumpkin	250 mL
1/2 cup	canned chickpeas, rinsed and drained	125 mL
1/2 cup	canned diced tomatoes, with juice	125 mL
1 tsp	crumbled dried sage	5 mL

1. In a medium saucepan, combine pumpkin, chickpeas, tomatoes with juice and sage; bring to a simmer. Cover and simmer until pumpkin is tender, about 15 minutes. Let cool.

2. Transfer to blender and purée on high speed to desired consistency.

**Nutritional Information
(Per 1/2-cup/125 mL Serving)**

Calories . . . . 46 Kcal
Total Carbohydrates . . . . 9 g
Fiber. . . . . 1 g
Fat. . . . . 1 g
Protein . . . . 2 g
Iron. . . . . 1 mg

Quick and Easy Quinoa

1 cup	quinoa	250 mL
2 cups	water or homemade vegetable stock (see page 62)	500 mL
¼ cup	grated Parmesan cheese	60 mL

Quinoa (pronounced "keen-wa") is a practical grain because it is easy to cook and is high in protein and minerals. Toasting it first gives it the best flavor.

1. In a large skillet, over medium-high heat, toast quinoa, shaking constantly, until golden, about 3 minutes. Add water and bring to a boil. Reduce heat to low and simmer, uncovered, for 12 to 15 minutes, or until liquid has been absorbed. Let cool slightly.

2. Transfer to blender, add cheese and purée on high speed until combined.

**Nutritional Information
(Per ¼-cup/60 mL Serving)**

Calories	103 Kcal
Total Carbohydrates	15 g
Fiber	2 g
Fat	2 g
Protein	7 g
Iron	2 mg

**MAKES ABOUT
2 CUPS (500 ML)**

*You are never too
young to love risotto!*

TIP

If your baby is over
eight months, serve
with chicken purée
for a complete meal.

Squash and Pepper Risotto

2 cups	water or homemade vegetable stock (see page 62)	500 mL
1/2 cup	Arborio or other short-grain rice	125 mL
1/2 cup	diced peeled butternut squash	125 mL
1/2 cup	chopped roasted red bell pepper	125 mL

1. In a medium saucepan, combine water, rice and squash; bring to a boil. Cover, reduce heat and simmer, stirring occasionally, until rice is very tender and most of the liquid has been absorbed, about 20 minutes. Stir in red pepper.

2. Transfer to blender and purée on high speed to desired consistency.

**Nutritional Information
(Per 1/4-cup/60 mL Serving)**

Calories	63 Kcal
Total Carbohydrates	12 g
Fiber	1 g
Fat	0 g
Protein	4 g
Iron	1 mg

Vegetable Paella

1 1/2 cups	water or homemade vegetable stock (see page 62)	375 mL
1/2 tsp	ground turmeric	2 mL
1 tbsp	olive oil	15 mL
1/4 cup	chopped onion	60 mL
1/2 cup	medium-grain rice, rinsed	125 mL
1/4 cup	chopped green bell pepper	60 mL
1/4 cup	chopped red bell pepper	60 mL
1/4 cup	frozen peas	60 mL

1. In a measuring cup, whisk together water and turmeric.

2. In a skillet, heat oil over medium-high heat. Add onion and cook, stirring, until tender, about 3 minutes. Stir in rice, green pepper, red pepper, peas and stock mixture; bring to a boil. Reduce heat and simmer, partially covered, until rice is tender and liquid is absorbed, about 15 minutes.

3. Transfer to blender and purée on high speed to desired consistency.

Nutritional Information (Per 1/4-cup/60 mL Serving)	
Calories	74 Kcal
Total Carbohydrates	11 g
Fiber	1 g
Fat	2 g
Protein	3 g
Iron	1 mg
Vitamin C	15 mg

MAKES ABOUT 2 CUPS (500 ML)

This version of the traditional Spanish dish is quick and simple.

TIP

Combining vitamin C–rich foods with iron-rich foods helps the body absorb more iron. Red peppers are rich in vitamin C, and enriched rice is a good source of iron.

Lean white fish has a very mild flavor and can be quickly prepared.

FOR OLDER KIDS

Spoon $\frac{1}{2}$ cup (125 mL) purée onto a split baked potato and sprinkle with shredded cheese. Bake in preheated 350°F (180°C) oven until potato is warmed through and cheese is melted, about 15 minutes.

Fish and Mushy Peas

1 cup	frozen sweet peas	250 mL
6 oz	skinless cod,* haddock or halibut fillet	175 g
$\frac{1}{2}$ cup	water or homemade vegetable stock (see page 62)	125 mL
1 tsp	freshly squeezed lemon juice	5 mL

* Nutritional information is for cod

1. Arrange peas in a medium saucepan. Place fish on top and pour water over fish. Cover and cook over medium heat until fish flakes easily when tested with a fork, about 10 minutes. Let cool.

2. Transfer to blender, add lemon juice and purée on high speed to desired consistency.

**Nutritional Information
(Per $\frac{1}{2}$-cup/125 mL Serving)**

Calories . . . . 69 Kcal
Total Carbohydrates . . . . 5 g
Fiber . . . . 2 g
Fat . . . . 0 g
Protein . . . . 11 g
Iron . . . . 1 mg

Cod with Celery and Peppers

6 oz	skinless cod fillet	175 g
1	stalk celery, diced	1
1 cup	diced red bell pepper	250 mL
1 cup	water	250 mL
1/4 cup	long-grain white rice	60 mL

1. In a medium saucepan, combine cod, celery, red pepper, water and rice; bring to a boil over medium-high heat. Cover, reduce heat and simmer until fish flakes easily when tested with a fork and rice is tender, about 15 minutes. Let cool.

2. Transfer to blender and purée on high speed to desired consistency.

Nutritional Information (Per 1/2-cup/125 mL Serving)	
Calories	90 Kcal
Total Carbohydrates	12 g
Fiber	1 g
Fat	0 g
Protein	9 g
Iron	1 mg
Vitamin C	72 mg

MAKES ABOUT 2 CUPS (500 ML)

Celery brings great flavor to this delicate dish.

127

8

**MAKES ABOUT
2 CUPS (500 ML)**

*The mild flavor of
this purée is especially
pleasing to young
palates.*

TIP

Cooking the leek and
corn first gives them
a mild, sweet flavor.
If you're in a hurry,
omit the oil and cook
the leek, corn, fish and
water in a covered pot
over medium-high heat
until leek is tender and
fish flakes easily when
tested with a fork, about
8 minutes. Purée on
high speed to desired
consistency.

Haddock, Corn and Leeks

2 tsp	olive oil	10 mL
½ cup	chopped leek, white and light green parts only	125 mL
1 cup	frozen sweet corn	250 mL
6 oz	skinless haddock fillet	175 g
¼ cup	water	60 mL

1. In a nonstick skillet, heat oil over medium-high heat. Add leeks and cook, stirring, until tender but not browned, about 3 minutes. Add corn and cook for 2 minutes more. Arrange haddock on top of leek-corn mixture and pour in water; cover and cook until fish flakes easily when tested with a fork, about 8 minutes. Let cool.

2. Transfer to blender and purée on high speed to desired consistency.

**Nutritional Information
(Per ½-cup/125 mL Serving)**

Calories . . . . 100 Kcal
Total Carbohydrates . . . . 10 g
Fiber . . . . 1 g
Fat . . . . 3 g
Protein . . . . 9 g
Iron . . . . 1 mg

Cheesy Salmon and Broccoli Dinner

1 cup	broccoli florets	250 mL
1	small potato, peeled and diced	1
8 oz	skinless salmon fillets	250 g
½ cup	full-fat (3.5% M.F.) milk	125 mL
¼ cup	shredded Cheddar cheese	60 mL

1. Arrange potatoes and broccoli in a medium saucepan. Lay salmon fillets on top and pour milk over salmon; bring to a boil over medium-high heat. Cover, reduce heat and simmer for 15 to 20 minutes, or until vegetables are tender and fish flakes easily when tested with a fork. Let cool.

2. Transfer to blender, add cheese and purée on high speed to desired consistency.

MAKES ABOUT 2 CUPS (500 ML)

Oily fish, such as salmon, are an excellent source of iron. Iron is absorbed more easily when combined with vitamin C, which in this recipe is provided by the broccoli.

Nutritional Information
(Per ½-cup/125 mL Serving)

Calories	133 Kcal
Total Carbohydrates	6 g
Fiber	1 g
Fat	5 g
Protein	15 g
Iron	1 mg
Vitamin C	21 mg

VARIATION

For the ultimate in nutritional density, substitute an equal amount of blanched Swiss chard for the spinach.

Spinach, Salmon and Rice

2 tsp	olive oil	10 mL
¼ cup	chopped onion	60 mL
½ cup	long-grain white rice	125 mL
1 cup	water (approx.)	250 mL
1 cup	chopped fresh spinach	250 mL
4 oz	skinless salmon fillet	125 g
1 tsp	freshly squeezed lemon juice	5 mL

1. In a medium saucepan, heat oil over medium-high heat. Add onion and cook, stirring, until tender but not browned, about 3 minutes.

2. Add rice and stir until coated with oil. Stir in water and bring to a boil. Cover, reduce heat, and simmer until most of the water has been absorbed and rice is slightly tender, about 15 minutes.

3. Arrange spinach and salmon on top of rice; cover and continue to cook until spinach is wilted and salmon flakes easily when tested with a fork, about 10 minutes. Let sit, covered, for 10 minutes.

4. Transfer to blender, add lemon juice and purée on high speed to desired consistency, adding more water if necessary.

**Nutritional Information
(Per ½-cup/125 mL Serving)**

Calories	143 Kcal
Total Carbohydrates	20 g
Fiber	1 g
Fat	3 g
Protein	8 g
Iron	1 mg

Tilapia, Celery and Tomatoes

1 tbsp	olive oil	15 mL
½ cup	thinly sliced celery	125 mL
½ cup	sliced green onions	125 mL
½ cup	diced tomato	125 mL
½ tsp	dried dillweed	2 mL
4 oz	skinless tilapia fillet	175 g
½ cup	water	125 mL

1. In a medium saucepan, heat oil over medium-high heat. Add celery, green onions and tomato; cook, stirring occasionally, until celery is tender, about 5 minutes. Add tilapia and water; cover and cook until fish flakes easily when tested with a fork, about 5 minutes. Let cool.

2. Transfer to blender and purée on high speed until smooth.

Nutritional Information
(Per ½-cup/125 mL Serving)

Calories . . . . .64 Kcal
Total Carbohydrates . . . . .3 g
Fiber. . . . . .1 g
Fat. . . . . .4 g
Protein. . . . . .6 g
Iron. . . . . .0 mg

MAKES ABOUT 2 CUPS (500 ML)

The sweet flavor of this delicate white fish is a great way to introduce fish to your little one's diet.

VARIATION

Substitute halibut, orange roughy or cod for the tilapia.

Trout, Zucchini and Potatoes

The mild flavor of zucchini blends well with tender pink trout.

TIP

The pink flesh of the trout gives this savory purée a beautiful color, but other fish can be substituted and cooked in the same manner.

1	medium Yukon gold potato, peeled and diced	1
1	zucchini, diced	1
6 oz	trout fillet	175 g
	Water	

1. Arrange potato and zucchini in a medium saucepan. Lay trout on top, skin side down, and add enough water to almost cover potato and zucchini; cover and bring to a boil over medium-high heat. Reduce heat and simmer until potatoes are tender and trout flakes easily when tested with a fork, about 15 minutes. Let cool.

2. Remove skin from trout. Transfer to blender with potato-zucchini mixture and cooking liquid; purée on high speed, adding more water if necessary, until smooth.

**Nutritional Information
(Per ½-cup/125 mL Serving)**

Calories . . . . 96 Kcal
Total Carbohydrates . . . . 7 g
Fiber . . . . 1 g
Fat . . . . 3 g
Protein . . . . 10 g
Iron . . . . 1 mg

Avocado with Chicken

8 oz	boneless skinless chicken breast, cut in strips	250 g
1	avocado, peeled, pitted and sliced	1
1 tbsp	freshly squeezed lime juice	15 mL
¾ cup	homemade chicken stock or water	175 mL

1. Arrange chicken in a steamer basket fitted over a saucepan of boiling water. Cover and steam for 10 to 15 minutes, until chicken is no longer pink inside. Transfer to a cutting board and cut into 1-inch (2.5 cm) pieces. Let cool.

2. Transfer to blender and add avocado, lime juice and stock; purée on high speed to desired consistency.

3. *Make ahead:* Store in an airtight container in the refrigerator for up to 3 days. Do not freeze.

**Nutritional Information
(Per ½-cup/125 mL Serving)**

Calories	119 Kcal
Total Carbohydrates	3 g
Fiber	1 g
Fat	7 g
Protein	12 g
Iron	1 mg

**MAKES ABOUT
2 CUPS (500 ML)**

TIP

Cooking time depends on the thickness of the chicken breast.

FOR OLDER KIDS

Serve as a dip with baked whole wheat tortilla wedges.

*Couscous is a quick,
simple grain to prepare.
Choose the whole-wheat
variety to maximize
flavor and nutrition.*

Chicken and Citrus Couscous

1/2 cup	orange juice	125 mL
1 cup	water or homemade chicken stock (see page 62)	250 mL
1 cup	whole wheat couscous	250 mL
1 tbsp	olive oil	15 mL
6 oz	boneless skinless chicken breast, chopped	175 g
1/4 cup	chopped onion	60 mL
1 tbsp	chopped parsley	15 mL

1. In a medium saucepan, bring orange juice and water to a boil. Add couscous; cover and remove from heat. Let sit for 5 minutes or until most of the liquid is absorbed and couscous is tender. Let cool.

2. Meanwhile, in a skillet, heat oil over medium-high heat. Add chicken, turning, until evenly browned and no longer pink inside, about 5 minutes; transfer to a plate. Let cool. Add onion to skillet; cook, stirring, until tender, about 5 minutes.

3. Transfer onions, chicken and couscous to blender and purée on high speed to desired consistency. Sprinkle with parsley.

**Nutritional Information
(Per 1/2-cup/125 mL Serving)**

Calories . . . . 261 Kcal
Total Carbohydrates . . . . 38 g
Fiber . . . . 2 g
Fat . . . . 4 g
Protein . . . . 16 g
Iron . . . . 1 mg

Chicken Divine

1 tbsp	vegetable oil	15 mL
6 oz	boneless skinless chicken breast or thighs, chopped	175 g
½ cup	chopped onion	125 mL
½ cup	sliced white mushrooms	125 mL
1 cup	fresh broccoli florets	250 mL
¼ cup	shredded Cheddar cheese	60 mL

1. In a nonstick skillet, heat oil over medium-high heat. Add chicken, turning to brown evenly; transfer to a plate.

2. Add onion to skillet and cook, stirring, until tender, about 5 minutes. Add mushrooms and cook, stirring, until golden, about 7 minutes. Add water, broccoli and browned chicken; bring just to a boil. Cover, reduce heat and simmer until broccoli is very tender and chicken is no longer pink inside, about 10 minutes. Let cool.

3. Transfer to blender, sprinkle with cheese and purée on high speed to desired consistency.

MAKES ABOUT 2 CUPS (500 ML)

This flavor combination is a favorite no matter what your age!

TIP

If you prefer, you can use frozen broccoli instead of fresh. Place frozen broccoli in a strainer and run it under hot water for 30 seconds, then drain well before using. (That way, it won't add too much extra water.)

**Nutritional Information
(Per ½-cup/125 mL Serving)**

Calories	132 Kcal
Total Carbohydrates	3 g
Fiber	1 g
Fat	9 g
Protein	10 g
Iron	1 mg
Vitamin C	18 mg

*This purée has a great
balance of protein,
vegetables and
carbohydrates and
will help your child
get through an
action-packed day.*

TIP

For a flavor boost, add
a pinch of chili powder
to the carrot mixture.

Chicken Jambalaya

1 tbsp	olive oil	15 mL
6 oz	boneless skinless chicken breast, chopped	175 mL
1/2 cup	chopped peeled carrot	125 mL
1/4 cup	chopped onion	60 mL
1/4 cup	chopped celery	60 mL
1/4 cup	long-grain white rice	60 mL
1 cup	water or homemade chicken stock (see page 62)	250 mL
1	bay leaf	1

1. In a skillet, heat oil over medium-high heat. Add
chicken, turning to brown evenly; transfer to a
plate. Add carrot, onion and celery to skillet. Cook,
stirring, until onion is tender, about 5 minutes.
Stir in rice until coated with oil. Add water and
bay leaf. Bring to a boil and add chicken, with any
accumulated juices, back to skillet. Cover, reduce
heat to low and simmer until rice is tender and most
of the liquid has been absorbed, about 20 minutes.
Let cool. Discard bay leaf.

2. Transfer to blender and purée on high speed to
desired consistency.

**Nutritional Information
(Per 1/2-cup/125 mL Serving)**

Calories . . . . 134 Kcal
Total Carbohydrates . . . . 12 g
Fiber . . . . 1 g
Fat . . . . 4 g
Protein . . . . 12 g
Iron . . . . 1 mg

Chicken Pasta

1 cup	water or homemade chicken stock	250 mL
6 oz	boneless, skinless chicken, diced	175 g
½ cup	dried whole wheat pastini	125 mL

1. In a medium saucepan, bring water to boil over medium-high heat. Add chicken and pastini and simmer, uncovered, until chicken is cooked through and pasta is tender, about 10 minutes.

2. Transfer to blender and purée on high speed to desired consistency.

Nutritional Information
(Per ¼-cup/60 mL Serving)

Calories	69 Kcal
Total Carbohydrates	9 g
Fiber	1 g
Fat	0.6 g
Protein	7 g
Iron	0.6 mg

MAKES ABOUT 2 CUPS (500 ML)

Infants cannot resist the mellow taste of pasta and chicken.

**MAKES ABOUT
2 CUPS (500 ML)**

*Adding quinoa to this
chicken and vegetable
stew makes this a
fiber-rich meal for
little appetites.*

Chicken Quinoa Stew

2 cups	water or homemade chicken stock	500 mL
½ cup	quinoa	125 mL
6 oz	chopped boneless skinless chicken	175 g
¼ cup	finely chopped peeled carrots	60 mL
¼ cup	finely chopped celery	60 mL
¼ cup	finely chopped zucchini	60 mL

1. In medium saucepan, bring water to a boil over medium-high heat. Stir in quinoa, chicken, carrots, celery and zucchini. Reduce heat, cover and simmer until vegetables are very tender, chicken is cooked through and quinoa is cooked, about 15 minutes. Remove from heat, let stand, covered, for 10 minutes.

2. Transfer to blender and purée on high speed to desired consistency.

Nutritional Information (Per ¼-cup/60 mL Serving)	
Calories	42
Total Carbohydrates	8 g
Fiber	0.4 g
Fat	0.9 g
Protein	2 g
Iron	1 mg

Chicken with Brown Rice and Peas

1 tbsp	olive oil	15 mL
6 oz	boneless skinless chicken thighs, chopped	175 g
½ cup	chopped onion	125 mL
½ tsp	curry powder	2 mL
1½ cups	water or homemade chicken stock (see page 62)	375 mL
½ cup	long-grain brown rice, rinsed	125 mL
1 cup	frozen sweet peas	250 mL

1. In a medium saucepan, heat oil over medium-high heat. Add chicken, turning to brown evenly; transfer to a plate.

2. Add onion and curry powder to saucepan; cook, stirring, until onion is tender but not browned, about 3 minutes. Stir in water and rice; bring to a boil. Cover, reduce heat and simmer for 25 to 30 minutes, or until rice is almost tender. Add peas and browned chicken; simmer until chicken is no longer pink inside, about 10 minutes. Let cool.

3. Transfer to blender and purée on high speed to desired consistency.

Nutritional Information
(Per ½-cup/125 mL Serving)

Calories	193 Kcal
Total Carbohydrates	26 g
Fiber	3 g
Fat	5 g
Protein	11 g
Iron	2 mg

MAKES ABOUT 2 CUPS (500 ML)

A small amount of curry powder provides taste without heat, and will give little ones a palate for flavor!

TIP

Use whole-grain products such as brown rice and whole wheat bread to increase daily fiber intake.

**MAKES ABOUT
2 CUPS (500 ML)**

*This autumn harvest
dish is both sweet and
savory!*

VARIATION

Substitute turkey breast
for the chicken.

Chicken with Pumpkin

1 tbsp	olive oil	15 mL
6 oz	boneless skinless chicken breast, diced	175 g
1 cup	cubed peeled pie pumpkin	250 mL
1/2 cup	water or homemade chicken stock (see page 62)	125 mL
1/2 tsp	ground cinnamon	2 mL
1/4 tsp	ground allspice	1 mL
1/4 tsp	ground ginger	1 mL

1. In a medium saucepan, heat oil over medium heat. Add chicken, turning to brown evenly. Stir in pumpkin, water, cinnamon, allspice and ginger; bring to a boil. Cover, reduce heat and simmer until chicken is no longer pink inside and pumpkin is very tender, about 20 minutes. Let cool.

2. Transfer to blender and purée on high speed until smooth.

**Nutritional Information
(Per 1/2-cup/125 mL Serving)**

Calories . . . . 70 Kcal
Total Carbohydrates . . . . 3 g
Fiber . . . . 0 g
Fat . . . . 4 g
Protein . . . . 7 g
Iron . . . . 1 mg

Chicken with Red Pepper and Corn

1 tbsp	olive oil	15 mL
6 oz	boneless skinless chicken breast, chopped	175 g
1/4 cup	chopped onion	60 mL
1/2 cup	chopped roasted red bell pepper	125 mL
1/2 cup	frozen sweet corn	125 mL
1 tbsp	chopped fresh parsley	15 mL
1/2 cup	water or homemade chicken stock (see page 62)	125 mL

MAKES ABOUT 2 CUPS (500 ML)

Roasted red pepper adds smoky sweetness to chicken and corn.

1. In a skillet, heat oil over medium-high heat. Add chicken, turning to brown evenly; transfer to a plate.

2. Add onion to skillet and cook, stirring, until tender, about 5 minutes. Stir in pepper, corn and parsley; cook for 2 minutes. Add water and bring to a boil. Add browned chicken; cover, reduce heat and simmer until chicken is no longer pink inside and sauce thickens slightly. Let cool.

3. Transfer to blender and purée on high speed to desired consistency.

**Nutritional Information
(Per 1/2-cup/125 mL Serving)**

Calories	110 Kcal
Total Carbohydrates	6 g
Fiber	1 g
Fat	5 g
Protein	12 g
Iron	1 mg
Vitamin C	15 mg

If you think babies might not like basil, try this. Add a little minced garlic, too!

Pesto Chicken and Rice

2 cups	water	500 mL
¼ cup	brown rice	60 mL
¼ cup	chopped chicken	60 mL
2 tbsp	chopped basil	30 mL

1. In a medium saucepan, bring water and rice to a boil over medium-high heat. Add chicken and reduce heat, cover and simmer 20 minutes or until rice is tender and the chicken is cooked through. Let cool slightly.

2. Transfer to blender, add basil and purée on high speed to desired consistency.

**Nutritional Information
(Per ¼-cup/60 mL Serving)**

Calories . . . . 28 Kcal
Total Carbohydrates . . . . .5 g
Fiber . . . . 0.3 g
Fat . . . . 0.3 g
Protein . . . . .2 g
Iron . . . . 0.1 mg

Tropical Chicken

1 tbsp	vegetable oil	15 mL
1/4 cup	diced onion	60 mL
6 oz	boneless skinless chicken breast, chopped	175 g
1/4 cup	long-grain brown rice, rinsed	60 mL
1/2 cup	water or homemade chicken stock (see page 62)	125 mL
1/2 cup	diced peeled mango	125 mL

1. In a medium saucepan, heat oil over medium-high heat. Add onion and cook, stirring, until tender but not browned, about 5 minutes. Add chicken and cook, stirring, until lightly browned, about 7 minutes. Stir in rice and cook for 1 minute more. Stir in water and mango; bring to a boil. Cover, reduce heat and simmer until rice is tender and chicken is no longer pink inside, about 40 minutes. Let cool.

2. Transfer to blender and purée on high speed to desired consistency.

Nutritional Information
(Per 1/2-cup/125 mL Serving)

Calories	127 Kcal
Total Carbohydrates	13 g
Fiber	1 g
Fat	2 g
Protein	13 g
Iron	1 mg

MAKES ABOUT 2 CUPS (500 ML)

Ripe mango provides vitamins A and C and gives a mild, sweet flavor to this protein-rich dish. Mango skin can irritate a baby's mouth, so always peel before using.

TIP

Mangoes with shriveled skin tend to have fibrous flesh that is very acidic and unpleasant-tasting. Ripe mangoes have a sweet, fragrant aroma and yield slightly to the touch.

143

*Don't leave your
little one out over
the holidays!*

TIPS

Use 1 cup (250 mL)
chopped leftover
cooked turkey and add
it just before puréeing.

For a simple risotto,
stir into cooked rice
with a little homemade
chicken stock.

Turkey with Cranberries

1 tbsp	olive oil	15 mL
½ cup	diced peeled carrot	125 mL
½ cup	diced onion	125 mL
¼ cup	diced celery	60 mL
½ tsp	dried thyme	2 mL
6 oz	boneless skinless turkey breast, chopped	175 g
½ cup	water or homemade chicken stock (see page 62)	125 mL
¼ cup	fresh or frozen cranberries	60 mL

1. In a medium saucepan, heat oil over medium-high heat. Add carrot, onion, celery and thyme, stirring to combine. Cook, stirring, until vegetables are tender, about 5 minutes.

2. Add turkey and brown slightly. Stir in water and cranberries, scraping any brown bits from bottom of pan; bring to a boil. Cover, reduce heat and simmer until cranberries are very tender and turkey is no longer pink inside, about 30 minutes. Let cool.

3. Transfer to blender and purée on high speed to desired consistency.

**Nutritional Information
(Per ½-cup/125 mL Serving)**

Calories . . . . .115 Kcal
Total Carbohydrates . . . . .5 g
Fiber . . . . .1 g
Fat . . . . .6 g
Protein . . . . .10 g
Iron . . . . 1 mg

Pork with Prunes and Apples (page 153)

Cauliflower, Spinach and Sweet Potato Curry (page 161)

Fruit Custard (page 169)

Cheesy Broccoli and Ham Pasta (page 176)

Beefy Broccoli

6 oz	lean ground sirloin beef	175 g
2 cups	chopped broccoli florets and stems	500 mL
½ cup	water or homemade beef stock (see page 63)	125 mL

1. In a skillet, brown beef over medium-high heat, breaking up any large pieces, until no longer pink, about 7 minutes. Drain off fat and return beef to skillet.

2. Add broccoli and water; cover, reduce heat and simmer until broccoli is very tender, about 15 minutes. Let cool.

3. Transfer to blender and purée on high speed to desired consistency.

**Nutritional Information
(Per ½-cup/125 mL Serving)**

Calories	85 Kcal
Total Carbohydrates	3 g
Fiber	1 g
Fat	5 g
Protein	8 g
Iron	1 mg
Vitamin C	41 mg

**MAKES ABOUT
2 CUPS (500 ML)**

FOR OLDER KIDS

Stir into cooked egg noodles for a simple weeknight meal.

145

*This meat-based dish
sneaks in a little carrot
and cooks the pasta
right in the sauce.*

Spaghetti Bolognese

6oz	lean ground sirloin	175 g
2 tbsp	tomato paste	30 mL
1 cup	canned diced, no added salt tomatoes, with juices	250 mL
1 cup	water	250 mL
½ cup	finely chopped peeled carrots	125 mL
½ cup	dried whole wheat spaghetti, broken into small pieces	125 mL

1. In a non-stick skillet, brown sirloin over medium-high heat until no longer pink, breaking up any large pieces, about 7 minutes. Drain off fat.

2. Stir in tomato paste and cook one minute. Stir in tomatoes, water and carrots; bring to a boil. Cover and reduce heat; simmer until carrots are tender, about 15 minutes. Add spaghetti and cook until tender, about 10 minutes. Let cool.

3. Transfer to blender and purée on high speed to desired consistency.

**Nutritional Information
(Per ¼-cup/60 mL Serving)**

Calories	90 Kcal
Total Carbohydrates	10 g
Fiber	2 g
Fat	3 g
Protein	6 g
Iron	1 mg

Beef with Carrots and Orange

6 oz	lean ground sirloin beef	175 g
1 cup	cubed peeled carrots (about 2)	250 mL
1 cup	unsweetened orange juice	250 mL

MAKES ABOUT 2 CUPS (500 ML)

Carrots and orange juice are the perfect accompaniments to beef.

1. In a nonstick skillet, brown beef over medium-high heat, breaking up any large pieces, until no longer pink, about 7 minutes. Drain off fat and return beef to skillet.

2. Add carrots and orange juice; bring to a boil. Cover, reduce heat and simmer until carrots are very tender, about 20 minutes. Let cool.

3. Transfer to blender and purée on high speed to desired consistency.

**Nutritional Information
(Per ½-cup/125 mL Serving)**

Calories	141 Kcal
Total Carbohydrates	10 g
Fiber	1 g
Fat	7 g
Protein	11 g
Iron	1 mg
Vitamin C	34 mg

**MAKES ABOUT
2 CUPS (500 ML)**

*Start this family
favorite from the
beginning!*

FOR OLDER KIDS

Spoon into a
hollowed-out whole
wheat dinner roll
and sprinkle with
shredded cheese. Bake
in preheated 350°F
(180°C) oven until
cheese is melted, about
5 minutes.

Spoon ½ cup (125 mL)
chili onto a split baked
sweet potato and
sprinkle with shredded
Cheddar cheese. Bake in
preheated 350°F (180°C)
oven until cheese is
melted and potato is
warmed through, about
15 minutes. Top with
sour cream and sliced
green onions.

Chili for Beginners

6 oz	lean ground sirloin beef	175 g
1 cup	canned diced tomatoes, with juice	250 mL
½ cup	rinsed and drained canned red kidney beans	125 mL
¼ cup	diced green bell pepper	60 mL
¼ cup	frozen corn	60 mL

1. In a skillet, brown beef over medium-high heat, breaking up any large pieces, until no longer pink, about 7 minutes. Drain off fat and return beef to skillet.

2. Add tomatoes with juice, kidney beans, green pepper and corn. Cover, reduce heat and simmer for 15 minutes, until vegetables are very tender. Let cool.

3. Transfer to blender and purée on high speed to desired consistency.

**Nutritional Information
(Per ½-cup/125 mL Serving)**

Calories . . . . 117 Kcal
Total Carbohydrates . . . . 10 g
Fiber . . . . 3 g
Fat . . . . 5 g
Protein . . . . 8 g
Iron . . . . 1 mg

Shepherd's Pie

1	small Yukon gold potato, peeled and cubed	1
6 oz	lean ground sirloin beef	175 g
¼ cup	chopped onion	60 mL
¼ cup	chopped peeled carrot	60 mL
¼ cup	frozen peas	60 mL
¼ cup	frozen corn	60 mL

1. Place potato in a small saucepan of salted water and bring to a boil over medium-high heat; cook potato until tender, about 15 minutes. Drain.

2. Meanwhile, in a skillet, brown beef over medium-high heat, breaking up any large pieces, until no longer pink, about 7 minutes. Drain off fat and return to skillet. Add onion, carrot, peas and corn; cook, stirring occasionally, until onion and carrot are tender, about 10 minutes. Let cool.

3. Transfer to blender, add potato and purée on high speed to desired consistency.

Nutritional Information
(Per ½-cup/125 mL Serving)

Calories	117 Kcal
Total Carbohydrate	9 g
Fiber	2 g
Fat	6 g
Protein	7 g
Iron	1 mg

MAKES ABOUT 2 CUPS (500 ML)

You're never too young to fall in love with comfort foods!

VARIATION

Substitute ground pork or chicken for the beef.

TIP

Add homemade vegetable stock or more homemade chicken stock to make a great soup for the whole family.

Ham and Split Peas

2 tsp	olive oil	10 mL
1	carrot, peeled and diced	1
1	celery stalk, diced	1
½	onion, diced	½
½ cup	diced cooked ham (about 4 oz/125 g)	125 mL
1 cup	water or homemade chicken stock (see page 62)	250 mL
½ cup	dried split yellow peas, rinsed	125 mL

1. In a medium saucepan, heat oil over medium-high heat. Add carrot, celery, onion and ham; cook, stirring occasionally, until carrots are tender, about 7 minutes.

2. Add water and peas; cover, reduce heat and simmer until peas are tender, about 45 minutes. Let cool.

3. Transfer to blender and purée on high speed until smooth.

**Nutritional Information
(Per ½-cup/125 mL Serving)**

Calories . . . . 160 Kcal
Total Carbohydrates . . . . 19 g
Fiber . . . . 7 g
Fat . . . . 4 g
Protein . . . . 12 g
Iron . . . . 2 mg

Ham with Swiss Chard and Potatoes

1 tbsp	olive oil	15 mL
¼ cup	sliced onion	60 mL
½ cup	diced cooked ham (about 4 oz/125 g)	125 mL
1	small potato, peeled and cubed	1
2 cups	chopped Swiss chard	500 mL
½ cup	homemade vegetable stock (see page 62) (approx. quantity)	125 mL

MAKES ABOUT 2 CUPS (500 ML)

This hearty winter purée will keep your little one satisfied all day!

1. In a medium saucepan, heat oil over medium-high heat. Add onion and cook, stirring, until tender but not browned, about 5 minutes. Add ham and cook, stirring, until lightly browned, about 3 minutes. Stir in potato, Swiss chard and stock. Cover, reduce heat and simmer until potato is tender, about 15 minutes. Let cool.

2. Transfer to blender and purée on high speed to desired consistency, adding more stock if necessary.

Nutritional Information
(Per ½-cup/125 mL Serving)

Calories	89 Kcal
Total Carbohydrates	6 g
Fiber	1 g
Fat	5 g
Protein	5 g
Iron	1 mg

8

*Classic autumn flavors
combine to make a
savory dish sure to
please baby's palate.*

TIP

Golden Delicious
apples are an ideal
cooking apple because
they retain their flavor
when cooked.

Pork with Apples and Cabbage

1 tbsp	vegetable oil	15 mL
½ cup	diced onion	125 mL
8 oz	boneless pork loin chops, sliced	250 g
1	apple, peeled, cored and cubed	1
1 cup	shredded Savoy cabbage	250 mL
½ cup	sweetened apple juice or water (approx.)	125 mL

1. In a nonstick skillet, heat oil over medium-high heat. Add onion and cook, stirring, until tender but not browned, about 5 minutes. Add pork, turning to brown evenly. Add apple and cabbage; cook, stirring occasionally, for 5 minutes.

2. Pour apple juice into skillet; cover and cook, stirring occasionally, until cabbage and apple are very tender and pork is no longer pink inside, about 20 minutes. Let cool.

3. Transfer to blender and purée on high speed to desired consistency, adding more apple juice if necessary.

**Nutritional Information
(Per ½-cup/125 mL Serving)**

Calories . . . . .137 Kcal
Total Carbohydrates . . . . .10 g
Fiber. . . . . .2 g
Fat. . . . . .6 g
Protein . . . . .11 g
Iron. . . . . .1 mg

Pork with Prunes and Apples

¼ cup	pitted prunes	60 mL
½ cup	sweetened apple juice	125 mL
2 tsp	olive oil	10 mL
6 oz	boneless pork loin chop, sliced	175 g
¼ cup	sliced onion	60 mL
1	apple, peeled, cored and sliced	1

1. In a small bowl, pour apple juice over prunes; let sit for 15 minutes, until slightly softened.

2. Meanwhile, in a skillet, heat oil over medium-high heat. Add pork, turning to brown evenly. Transfer to a plate.

3. Add onion to skillet and cook, stirring, until tender and golden, about 5 minutes. Add apple and cook, stirring, for 5 minutes more. Stir in prunes with juice and browned pork; cover, reduce heat and simmer until apple and prunes are very tender and pork is no longer pink inside, about 10 minutes. Let cool.

4. Transfer to blender and purée on high speed to desired consistency.

MAKES ABOUT 2 CUPS (500 ML)

This purée is packed full of fruit and fiber to keep your little one "moving"!

TIP

If constipation is an issue, increase the prunes to ½ cup (125 mL) and omit the onions.

**Nutritional Information
(Per ½-cup/125 mL Serving)**

Calories	120 Kcal
Total Carbohydrates	16 g
Fiber	2 g
Fat	4 g
Protein	6 g
Iron	1 mg

This is simple and delicious. Stir it into cooked pasta for older kids.

TIP

If you don't have a non-stick skillet, heat 2 tsp (10 mL) of oil in your pan when you brown the veal.

Veal Ragu

6 oz	lean ground veal	175 g
1 cup	canned, diced, no added salt tomatoes, with juice	250 mL
½ cup	cubed peeled carrots	125 mL

1. In a non-stick skillet, cook veal over medium-high heat, breaking up large pieces, until no longer pink, about 7 minutes. Drain off fat.

2. Add tomatoes and carrots; bring to a boil. Cover and reduce heat and simmer until carrots are very tender, about 20 minutes. Let cool.

3. Transfer to blender and purée on high speed to desired consistency.

**Nutritional Information
(Per ¼-cup/60 mL Serving)**

Calories . . . . 40 Kcal
Total Carbohydrates . . . . 2 g
Fiber . . . . 0.5 g
Fat . . . . 2 g
Protein . . . . 4 g
Iron . . . . 0.5 mg

Veal and Carrots

6 oz	lean ground veal	175 g
1 cup	cubed peeled carrots	250 mL
1½ cups	water or homemade chicken stock	375 mL

1. In non-stick skillet, brown veal over medium high-heat, breaking up any large pieces, until no longer pink, about 7 minutes. Drain off fat.

2. Add carrots and water; bring to a boil. Cover and reduce heat and simmer until carrots are very tender, about 20 minutes. Let cool.

3. Transfer to blender and purée on high speed to desired consistency.

MAKES ABOUT 2 CUPS (500 ML)

Veal is a lean protein that has a great mild flavor and pairs very well with root veggies.

Nutritional Information
(Per ¼-cup/60 mL Serving)

Calories	36 Kcal
Total Carbohydrates	2 g
Fiber	0.5 g
Fat	2 g
Protein	4 g
Iron	0.3 mg

Many little ones will reject meat, especially as they reach toddlerhood. Tofu provides a nutritious alternative and requires minimal effort to prepare. It has a mild, nutty flavor that can be disguised by anything it is cooked with — perfect for babies. Try it!

Tofu

| 1 cup | cubed firm tofu (about 4 oz/125 g) | 250 mL |

1. Place tofu in blender and purée on high speed until smooth.

**Nutritional Information
(Per ¼-cup/60 mL Serving)**

Calories . . . . 49 Kcal
Total Carbohydrates . . . . 2 g
Fiber . . . . 0 g
Fat. . . . . 3 g
Protein . . . . 5 g
Iron. . . . . 1 mg

Meal Plans

At this age, your child can start to eat dairy foods such as yogurt and cheese, as well as adapted table food: diced fruits and cooked vegetables, tender chopped meats and casseroles with noodles cut up. Do not purée food until it is perfectly smooth — leave a few lumps to help your baby discover new textures. See the introduction for more information on these meal plans. Please note that these amounts are just suggestions. All babies are different and require different amounts of food. Let your baby eat until he or she turns away or appears full.

MEAL Plan for babies 9 months and older

MEAL	1	2	3
Breakfast	• ½ cup (125 mL) Power Yogurt with Fruit and Iron-Fortified Infant Cereal (page 180) • Breast or formula feeding	• ½ cup (125 mL) Fruity Breakfast Rice (page 170) • Breast or formula feeding	• ½ cup (125 mL) prepared iron-fortified infant cereal • ¼ cup (60 mL) Avocado Banana Yogurt (page 168) • Breast or formula feeding
Snack	• ¼ cup (60 mL) Blueberries (page 46) • ¼ cup (60 mL) puffed rice cereal, dry • Water	• ¼ cup (60 mL) Mango (page 49) • Whole wheat toast with margarine • Water	• ¼ cup (60 mL) Fruit Custard (page 169) • ¼ tortilla spread with cream cheese • Water
Lunch	• ½ cup (125 mL) Chicken Stew (page 98) • Breast or formula feeding	• ½ cup (125 mL) Over-the-Top Applesauce (page 174) • Whole wheat toast with margarine • Breast or formula feeding	• ½ cup (125 mL) Sweet Potatoes and Cottage Cheese (page 169) • Breast or formula feeding

MEAL	1	2	3
Snack	• Animal-shaped cookie • Sliced grapes • Water	• 1/4 cup (60 mL) puffed rice cereal, dry • Diced fresh peaches • Water	• 1/2 cup (125 mL) Mango, Banana and Cottage Cheese (page 173) • Water
Supper	• 1/2 cup (125 mL) Turkey with Cranberries (page 144) • 1/4 cup (60 mL) Mango (page 49) • Breast or formula feeding	• 1/2 cup (125 mL) Shepherd's Pie (page 149) • 1/4 cup (60 mL) Apples (page 43) • Breast or formula feeding	• 1/2 cup (125 mL) Cheesy Broccoli and Ham Pasta (page 176) • Diced ripe pears • Breast or formula feeding
Snack	• Breast or formula feeding on demand	• Breast or formula feeding on demand	• Breast or formula feeding on demand

*Cauliflower mellows
out the flavor of
broccoli without
compromising
nutrients or taste.*

TIP

To increase the fiber
content of vegetable
dishes, sprinkle with
1 tbsp (15 mL) wheat
germ before puréeing.

To maintain its
freshness, store wheat
germ in an airtight
container in the
refrigerator for up to
6 months or in the
freezer for up to 1 year.

Broccoli and Cauliflower Gratin

1 cup	broccoli florets	250 mL
1 cup	cauliflower florets	250 mL
1 cup	water or homemade vegetable stock (see page 62)	250 mL
½ cup	shredded Cheddar cheese	125 mL

1. In a medium saucepan, combine broccoli, cauliflower and water; bring to a boil. Cover, reduce heat and simmer until vegetables are very tender, about 15 minutes. Let cool.

2. Transfer to blender, add cheese and purée on high speed until smooth.

**Nutritional Information
(Per ¼-cup/60 mL Serving)**

Calories . . . . 40 Kcal
Total Carbohydrates . . . . 1 g
Fiber . . . . 1 g
Fat. . . . . 2 g
Protein . . . . 4 g
Iron. . . . . 0 mg

Cauliflower, Spinach and Sweet Potato Curry

MAKES ABOUT 2 CUPS (500 ML)

Don't be afraid to begin introducing new flavors. Mild curry paste adds flavor without heat in this nutritious meal.

TIP

Serve over cooked basmati rice for the whole family.

1 tbsp	vegetable oil	15 mL
¼ cup	chopped onion	60 mL
1 tsp	black mustard seeds	5 mL
2 tsp	mild curry paste	10 mL
1 cup	full-fat (3.5% M.F.) milk	250 mL
½ cup	water or homemade vegetable or chicken stock (see page 62)	125 mL
1 cup	chopped cauliflower	250 mL
½ cup	chopped peeled sweet potato	125 mL
1 cup	chopped fresh spinach	250 mL

1. In a skillet, heat oil over medium-high heat. Add onion and cook, stirring, until tender, about 5 minutes. Add mustard seeds and curry paste; cook, stirring, for 1 minute. Stir in milk and water; bring just to a boil. Add cauliflower and sweet potato. Cover, reduce heat to low and simmer until vegetables are very tender, about 15 minutes. Stir in spinach, remove from heat and let cool.

2. Transfer to blender and purée on high speed to desired consistency.

Nutritional Information
(Per ¼-cup/60 mL Serving)

Calories	58 Kcal
Total Carbohydrates	5 g
Fiber	1 g
Fat	3 g
Protein	2 g
Iron	Trace

9

TIPS

Substitute an equal
amount of plain yogurt
for the sour cream.

For a little zip, add
$\frac{1}{4}$ tsp (1 mL) grated
orange zest.

Creamy Sweet Corn

1 tbsp	butter	15 mL
2 cups	frozen corn kernels, thawed	500 mL
$\frac{1}{2}$ cup	water	125 mL
$\frac{1}{4}$ cup	sour cream	60 mL

1. In a skillet, melt butter over medium-high heat. Add corn and stir to coat. Add water. Cover, reduce heat to medium and cook until corn is very soft, about 10 minutes. Let cool.

2. Transfer to blender, add sour cream and purée on high speed until smooth.

**Nutritional Information
(Per $\frac{1}{4}$-cup/60 mL Serving)**

Calories . . . . 64 Kcal
Total Carbohydrates . . . . 9 g
Fiber . . . . 1 g
Fat . . . . 3 g
Protein . . . . 1 g
Iron . . . . Trace

Spinach and Tomatoes with Ricotta

1 tbsp	olive oil	15 mL
1	clove garlic, minced	1
½ cup	canned diced tomatoes, with juice	125 mL
2 cups	trimmed spinach	500 mL
¼ cup	ricotta cheese	60 mL
2 tsp	freshly squeezed lemon juice	10 mL

1. In a skillet, heat oil over medium heat. Add garlic and tomatoes with juice; cook until garlic is fragrant but not browned, about 2 minutes. Stir in spinach and cook until completely wilted, about 3 minutes. Let cool.

2. Transfer to blender and add ricotta and lemon juice; purée on high speed until smooth.

Nutritional Information
(Per ¼-cup/60 mL Serving)

Calories	35 Kcal
Total Carbohydrates	3 g
Fiber	0 g
Fat	3 g
Protein	1 g
Iron	0 mg

MAKES ABOUT 2 CUPS (500 ML)

Creamy ricotta balances the acidity of spinach and tomatoes.

TIPS

Fresh spinach is very sandy and must be washed thoroughly in a large basin of water. Change the water if necessary. Trim woody stems for even cooking.

Steaming spinach tends to bring out its bitterness. Instead, cook it in a covered saucepan, over high heat, in the liquid that remains on the leaves after washing.

FOR OLDER KIDS

Stir into cooked pasta.

*Surprise! The cheese
eliminates any
bitterness from the
spinach.*

Spinach Surprise

1 tbsp	olive oil	15 mL
¼ cup	minced onion	60 mL
1	package (10 oz/300 g) fresh spinach, tough stems removed	1
½ cup	half-and-half (10%) cream	125 mL
¼ cup	grated Parmesan cheese	60 mL

1. In a skillet, heat oil over medium-high heat. Add onion and cook, stirring, until tender, about 5 minutes. Add spinach and cream. Cover and cook until spinach has wilted, about 3 minutes. Remove from heat and let cool slightly.

2. Transfer to blender, add Parmesan and purée on high speed until just combined.

**Nutritional Information
(Per ¼-cup/60 mL Serving)**

Calories	56 Kcal
Total Carbohydrates	2 g
Fiber	1 g
Fat	4 g
Protein	3 g
Iron	1 mg

Sweet Potatoes and Cottage Cheese

2 cups	cubed peeled sweet potatoes (about 2 small)	500 mL
½ cup	unsweetened apple juice	125 mL
½ cup	small-curd cottage cheese	125 mL

1. Arrange sweet potatoes in a steamer basket fitted over a medium saucepan of boiling water. Cover and steam until potatoes are very tender, about 20 minutes. Let cool.

2. Transfer to blender and add apple juice and cottage cheese; purée on high speed until well combined.

Nutritional Information
(Per ¼-cup/60 mL Serving)

Calories . . . . 46 Kcal
Total Carbohydrates . . . . 8 g
Fiber . . . . 1 g
Fat . . . . 0 g
Protein . . . . 2 g
Iron . . . . 0 mg

MAKES ABOUT 2 CUPS (500 ML)

Adding cottage cheese to vegetables makes for a protein-rich meal.

9

*Cauliflower is the
most easily digestible
member of the
cabbage family and
is an excellent source
of vitamin C and
potassium.*

Tomato, Cauliflower and Cheese

2 tsp	olive oil	10 mL
¼ cup	chopped onion	60 mL
1 cup	cauliflower florets	250 mL
½ cup	canned diced tomatoes, with juice	125 mL
¼ cup	shredded Cheddar cheese	60 mL

1. In a skillet, heat oil over medium-high heat. Add onion and cook, stirring occasionally, until tender, but not browned, about 5 minutes. Add cauliflower and tomatoes with juice. Cover, reduce heat and simmer until cauliflower is tender, about 10 minutes. Let cool.

2. Transfer to blender, add cheese and purée on high speed until smooth.

**Nutritional Information
(Per ¼-cup/60 mL Serving)**

Calories . . . . 32 Kcal
Total Carbohydrates . . . . 2 g
Fiber . . . . 1 g
Fat . . . . 2 g
Protein . . . . 1 g
Iron . . . . 0 mg

Vegetable Frittata

Preheat oven to 325°F (160°C)
8-inch (2 L) square glass baking dish, brushed
with vegetable oil

4	egg yolks	4
¼ cup	vegetable purée (any flavor), thawed	60 mL
¼ cup	full-fat (3.5% M.F.) milk	60 mL
¼ cup	shredded Cheddar cheese	60 mL

1. Place egg yolks, vegetable purée and milk in blender; purée on high speed until well combined and smooth.

2. Pour egg mixture into prepared baking dish and sprinkle with cheese. Bake in preheated oven until eggs are puffed and set, about 35 minutes. Let cool slightly. Cut into bite-size pieces and serve.

Nutritional Information (Per Serving)

Calories	117 Kcal
Total Carbohydrates	2 g
Fiber	0 g
Fat	10 g
Protein	6 g
Iron	1 mg

MAKES 4 SERVINGS

Use up leftover vegetable purée with this simple main dish that can be cut into portable pieces.

Avocado Banana Yogurt

1	banana	1
1	avocado, peeled and pitted	1
1/2 cup	plain yogurt	125 mL

1. Place banana, avocado and yogurt in blender and purée on high speed until smooth.

Nutritional Information (Per 1/4-cup/60 mL Serving)
Calories . . . . 65 Kcal
Total Carbohydrates . . . . 9 g
Fiber . . . . 1 g
Fat . . . . 3 g
Protein . . . . 1 g
Iron . . . . 0 mg

Banana Cherry Blast

1	very ripe banana	1
1/2 cup	pitted sour cherries	125 mL
1/4 cup	cherry juice (drained from cherries)	60 mL
1/2 cup	plain yogurt	125 mL

1. Place banana, cherries, cherry juice and yogurt in blender and purée on high speed until smooth.

Nutritional Information (Per 1/2-cup/125 mL Serving)
Calories . . . . 149 Kcal
Total Carbohydrates . . . . 31 g
Fiber . . . . 2 g
Fat . . . . 2 g
Protein . . . . 3 g
Iron . . . . 0 mg

Nutty Choco' Monkey (page 186)

Orange Banana Smoothie (page 187)

Nutty Waffles (page 189)

Breakfast Toast Strips (page 193)

Fruit Custard

Preheat oven to 350°F (180°C)
Four 6-oz (175 mL) ramekins
Large baking pan

2	egg yolks	2
½ cup	full-fat (3.5% M.F.) milk	125 mL
¼ cup	sliced banana	60 mL
¼ cup	raspberries	60 mL
½ tsp	grated lemon zest	2 mL

1. Place egg yolks, milk, banana, raspberries and zest in blender; purée on high speed until very smooth.

2. Pour into ramekins and arrange in baking pan. Pour in boiling water to reach halfway up the sides of the ramekins. Bake in preheated oven until custard is set, about 30 minutes. Serve warm or chilled.

3. *Make ahead:* Store in an airtight container in the refrigerator for up to 3 days.

Nutritional Information (Per Serving)	
Calories	66 Kcal
Total Carbohydrates	6 g
Fiber	1 g
Fat	4 g
Protein	3 g
Iron	Trace

MAKES 4 SERVINGS

A simple creamy dessert just for baby!

TIP

Replace the banana and raspberries with ½ cup (125 mL) of any of your little one's favorite fruit purées from previous chapters.

*The rice is a nice
change from oatmeal.*

TIP

Sprinkle with a teaspoon
of wheat germ for an
extra fiber boost!

VARIATION

Replace bananas and
strawberries with any
fruit your child enjoys.

Fruity Breakfast Rice

1/2 cup	medium-grain brown rice, rinsed	125 mL
1/2 cup	full-fat (3.5% M.F.) milk (approx.)	125 mL
1/2 cup	water	125 mL
1 tsp	vanilla	5 mL
1/2 tsp	ground cinnamon	2 mL
1/2 tsp	salt	2 mL
1/4 cup	sliced banana	60 mL
1/4 cup	chopped strawberries	60 mL

1. In a medium saucepan, combine rice, milk, water, vanilla, cinnamon and salt. Bring to a boil over medium-high heat. Cover, reduce heat to low and simmer, stirring occasionally, until liquid has been absorbed, about 50 minutes. Let cool.

2. Transfer to blender and add bananas and strawberries; purée on high speed until smooth. Serve warm with additional milk, if desired, for added creaminess.

**Nutritional Information
(Per 1/4-cup/60 mL Serving)**

Calories . . . . 108 Kcal
Total Carbohydrates . . . . 17 g
Fiber . . . . 4 g
Fat . . . . 2 g
Protein . . . . 6 g
Iron . . . . 2 mg

Fruity Cottage Cheese

¹/₂ cup	drained and rinsed canned mandarin orange segments	125 mL
¹/₂ cup	sliced strawberries	125 mL
¹/₂ cup	sliced peach	125 mL
¹/₂ cup	2% cottage cheese	125 mL
¹/₄ cup	unsweetened peach nectar	60 mL

MAKES ABOUT 2 CUPS (500 ML)

Adding cottage cheese to fruit or vegetables is a quick way to get in some protein on action-packed days (aren't they all?).

1. Place oranges, strawberries, peach, cottage cheese and peach nectar in blender and purée on high speed until blended.

2. *Make ahead:* Store in an airtight container in the refrigerator for up to 3 days. Do not freeze.

TIP

Use thawed frozen fruit mixes when fresh fruits aren't available.

**Nutritional Information
(Per ¹/₄-cup/60 mL Serving)**

Calories	30 Kcal
Total Carbohydrates	5 g
Fiber	1 g
Fat	0 g
Protein	2 g
Iron	0 mg

9

**MAKES ABOUT
2 CUPS (500 ML)**

*Adding your own fruit
purée to plain yogurt
is a much healthier
option than using
store-bought varieties.*

TIPS

The bacteria found in
plain yogurt, called
lactobacillus, works to
maintain a balance in
the intestinal tract. It
is easy for little systems
to digest. Avoid yogurts
with preservatives,
additives and coloring.

Avoid low-fat and
no-fat dairy products
for at least the first
two years of your
child's life. A child's
brain needs fat for
full development.

VARIATION

Use an equal amount
of any fruit you have
on hand for a different
flavor every day.

Lemon Raspberry Yogurt

½ cup	fresh or frozen raspberries	125 mL
1½ cups	vanilla-flavored yogurt	375 mL
	Grated zest and juice of 1 lemon	

1. Place raspberries, yogurt, lemon zest and lemon juice in blender and purée on high speed until smooth and well combined.

2. *Make ahead:* Store in an airtight container in the refrigerator for up to 1 week.

**Nutritional Information
(Per ¼-cup/60 mL Serving)**

Calories	34 Kcal
Total Carbohydrates	4 g
Fiber	1 g
Fat	2 g
Protein	2 g
Iron	0 mg

Mango, Banana and Cottage Cheese

1	banana	1
1	mango, peeled, pitted and cubed	1
½ cup	small-curd cottage cheese	125 mL

1. Place banana, mango and cottage cheese in blender and purée on high speed until smooth.

2. *Make ahead:* Store in an airtight container in the refrigerator for up to 3 days. Do not freeze.

**Nutritional Information
(Per ¼-cup/60 mL Serving)**

Calories	43 Kcal
Total Carbohydrates	8 g
Fiber	1 g
Fat	0 g
Protein	2 g
Iron	0 mg

**MAKES ABOUT
2 CUPS (500 ML)**

FOR OLDER KIDS

Serve as a dip with celery sticks and pieces of apple and pear.

9

*Fat is an essential
nutrient for your little
one's brain development.
Adding creamy ricotta
to a favorite fruit or
vegetable is a great way
to pack in calories when
they're going through
a growth spurt and
aren't eating as much
as you'd like.*

FOR OLDER KIDS

Serve over pound cake.

Over-the-Top Applesauce

4 cups	sliced peeled Golden Delicious apples (about 5)	1 L
½ cup	unsweetened apple juice	125 mL
¼ cup	ricotta or mascarpone cheese	60 mL
1 tsp	ground cinnamon	5 mL
½ tsp	grated lemon zest	2 mL
¼ tsp	ground ginger	1 mL
¼ tsp	ground nutmeg	1 mL

1. In a medium saucepan, combine apples with apple juice. Cover and simmer until apples break down and are very tender.

2. Transfer to blender and add ricotta, cinnamon, lemon zest, ginger and nutmeg; purée on high speed until smooth.

3. *Make ahead:* Store in an airtight container in the refrigerator for up to 1 week.

**Nutritional Information
(Per ¼-cup/60 mL Serving)**

Calories . . . . 46 Kcal
Total Carbohydrates . . . . 8 g
Fiber . . . . 1 g
Fat . . . . 1 g
Protein . . . . 1 g
Iron . . . . 0 mg

Cheesy Beef Casserole

6 oz	lean ground sirloin beef	175 g
1/4 cup	chopped onion	60 mL
1/2 cup	chopped peeled carrot	125 mL
1 cup	canned diced tomatoes, with juice	250 mL
1/2 cup	shredded Cheddar cheese	125 mL
	Water (optional)	

1. In a skillet, brown beef over medium-high heat, breaking up any large pieces, until no longer pink, about 5 minutes. Drain off fat and return beef to skillet. Add onion, carrot and tomatoes with juice. Cover and cook, stirring occasionally, until onion and carrot are tender, about 10 minutes. Let cool.

2. Transfer to blender, add cheese and purée on high speed to desired consistency, adding water if necessary.

**MAKES ABOUT
2 CUPS (500 ML)**

This quick skillet supper is good for every age!

FOR OLDER KIDS

Stir 1/2 cup (125 mL) purée into 1 cup (250 mL) cooked elbow noodles or any favorite pasta. This recipe is much more nutritious than packaged varieties.

**Nutritional Information
(Per 1/2-cup/125 mL Serving)**

Calories . . . . 200 Kcal
Total Carbohydrates . . . . 7 g
Fiber . . . . 1 g
Fat . . . . 13 g
Protein . . . . 15 g
Iron . . . . 2 mg

Kids can't get enough pasta, so get in the habit of making simple pasta dishes and avoid packaged varieties.

Cheesy Broccoli and Ham Pasta

$\frac{1}{2}$ cup	pastini	125 mL
1 cup	broccoli florets	250 mL
$\frac{1}{2}$ cup	diced cooked ham (about 4 oz/125 g)	125 mL
$\frac{1}{2}$ cup	herb-flavored cream cheese	125 mL

1. Add pastini and broccoli to a saucepan of boiling water; cook until tender, about 10 minutes. Drain, reserving $\frac{1}{4}$ cup (60 mL) of the cooking liquid. Stir in ham, cream cheese and reserved cooking liquid until well combined.

2. Transfer to blender and purée on high speed to desired consistency.

**Nutritional Information
(Per $\frac{1}{2}$-cup/125 mL Serving)**

Calories	206 Kcal
Total Carbohydrates	12 g
Fiber	1 g
Fat	13 g
Protein	9 g
Iron	1 mg
Vitamin C	24 mg

Fisherman's Pie

1	small Yukon gold potato, peeled and cubed	1
¼ cup	chopped onion	60 mL
4 oz	trout fillet (skin removed)	125 g
½ cup	frozen corn	125 mL
½ cup	broccoli florets	125 mL
¼ cup	shredded Cheddar cheese	60 mL

1. Place potato in a small saucepan of salted water. Bring to a boil over medium-high heat and cook until potato is tender, about 15 minutes. Drain.

2. Meanwhile, in a skillet, heat oil over medium-high heat. Add onion and cook until tender, about 5 minutes. Add trout, browning on both sides. Stir in corn and broccoli; cover and cook until fish flakes easily when pierced with a fork and broccoli is tender, about 5 minutes. Let cool.

3. Transfer to blender and add potatoes and cheese; purée on high speed to desired consistency.

**Nutritional Information
(Per ½-cup/125 mL Serving)**

Calories	63 Kcal
Total Carbohydrates	12 g
Fiber	1 g
Fat	0 g
Protein	4 g
Iron	1 mg

**MAKES ABOUT
2 CUPS (500 ML)**

Serve fish as often as you can to get your little one on the road to healthy eating.

VARIATION

Substitute salmon for the trout.

9

**MAKES ABOUT
2 CUPS (500 ML)**

Using short- or medium-grain rice gives a creamy texture without extra fat in this nutritious classic treat.

Creamy Brown Rice Pudding

¼ cup	short-grain brown rice, rinsed	60 mL
¼ cup	water	60 mL
1½ cups	full-fat (3.5% M.F.) milk	375 mL
¼ cup	packed brown sugar	60 mL
1 tbsp	vanilla	15 mL
¼ cup	currants (optional)	60 mL

1. In a small saucepan, combine brown rice and water; bring to a boil over medium-high heat. Cover, reduce heat to low and simmer until most of the liquid has been absorbed, about 20 minutes. Stir in milk, brown sugar, vanilla and currants (if using); increase heat to medium-high and bring to a boil, stirring often. Reduce heat to medium and simmer, stirring often, until rice is a porridge consistency, about 30 minutes. Let cool slightly.

2. Transfer to blender and purée on high speed to desired consistency.

Nutritional Information **(Per ¼-cup/60 mL Serving)**	
Calories	71 Kcal
Total Carbohydrates	12 g
Fiber	0 g
Fat	2 g
Protein	2 g
Iron	Trace

Barley with Apples and Dates

2	dates, pitted and chopped	2
1 cup	chopped peeled apples	250 mL
1 cup	full-fat (3.5% M.F.) milk	250 mL
½ cup	barley	125 mL

1. In a medium saucepan, over medium-high heat, bring dates, apples, milk and barley just to a boil. Cover, reduce heat to low and simmer until barley is tender, about 45 minutes. Let cool.

2. Transfer to blender and purée on high speed until smooth.

Nutritional Information
(Per ¼-cup/60 mL Serving)

Calories	74 Kcal
Total Carbohydrates	14 g
Fiber	2 g
Fat	1 g
Protein	3 g
Iron	Trace

MAKES ABOUT 2 CUPS (500 ML)

Barley is an excellent source of water-soluble fiber and is said to have anti-diarrheal properties.

TIP

Choose pearl barley — it doesn't need to be presoaked and cooks in half the time it takes pot barley.

**MAKES ABOUT
2 CUPS (500 ML)**

*Stirring a little cereal
into yogurt pumps up
the nutritional value of
this dish and makes a
great breakfast, snack
or dessert.*

Power Yogurt
with fruit and iron-fortified infant cereal

1 cup	full-fat (3.5% M.F.) plain yogurt	250 mL
1 cup	mixed fruit	250 mL
½ cup	chopped banana	125 mL
¼ cup	iron-fortified infant cereal	60 mL

1. In blender, combine yogurt, fruit, banana and cereal. Purée on high speed to desired consistency.

**Nutritional Information
(Per ¼-cup/60 mL Serving)**

Calories	19 Kcal
Total Carbohydrates	4 g
Fiber	2 g
Fat	0.1 g
Protein	0.3 g
Iron	1 mg

Polenta with Apricots

½ cup	dried apricots, chopped	125 mL
1½ cups	water or homemade chicken stock (see page 62)	375 mL
½ cup	cornmeal	125 mL
¼ cup	plain yogurt	60 mL

MAKES ABOUT 2 CUPS (500 ML)

Mild, creamy polenta blends beautifully with apricots and yogurt.

1. In a medium saucepan, bring apricots and water to a boil. Gradually stir in cornmeal until well combined. Reduce heat and simmer, stirring frequently, until mixture is creamy. Let cool slightly.

2. Transfer to blender, add yogurt and purée on high speed until smooth.

Nutritional Information (Per ¼-cup/60 mL Serving)

Calories	80 Kcal
Total Carbohydrates	12 g
Fiber	1 g
Fat	2 g
Protein	3 g
Iron	0 mg

*Add a little extra
protein to baby's
breakfast with a creamy
full-fat yogurt.*

TIP

Stir in puréed fruit if
desired.

Yogurty Oatmeal

½ cup	steel cut oats	125 mL
2 tbsp	ground flax seed	30 mL
1 cup	water	250 mL
½ cup	full-fat (3.5% M.F.) milk	125 mL
Pinch	cinnamon (optional)	Pinch
½ cup	full-fat (3.5% M.F.) plain yogurt	125 mL

1. In small saucepan, combine oats, flax seed and
   water. Bring to a boil over medium-high heat.
   Reduce heat and simmer, stirring often, until oats
   are tender and most of the liquid has been absorbed,
   about 20 minutes. Let cool slightly.

2. Transfer to blender with milk, cinnamon and
   yogurt. Purée on high speed to desired consistency.

**Nutritional Information
(Per ¼-cup/60 mL Serving)**

Calories . . . . 58 Kcal
Total Carbohydrates . . . . 9 g
Fiber . . . . 2 g
Fat . . . . 2 g
Protein . . . . 2 g
Iron . . . . 0.5 mg

FOOD FOR BABIES

Twelve Months and Older

Meal Plans

At this age, formula-fed babies can be switched to full-fat (3.5% M.F.) milk. Breastfed babies can continue breastfeeding into their second year or can be switched to whole milk. Toddlers eat erratically. You may have more success if you feed when your child is hungry rather than at particular times. Remember to include all the food groups: grain products, vegetables and fruits, milk products and meat and alternatives. Each food group provides unique nutrients, so it is important to offer your child a variety of foods from each food group every day. A good rule of thumb is to aim for three of the four food groups at each meal and one or two of the food groups at each snack. This will ensure that your child gets all the nutrients he or she needs to grow and develop. See the introduction for more information on these meal plans. Please note that the amounts are just suggestions. All toddlers are different and require different amounts of food. It may take over 10 exposures to a food before a toddler will eat it. Be patient.

MEAL Plan for babies 12 months and older

MEAL	1	2	3
Breakfast	• Breakfast Toast Strips (page 193) with Fruity Yogurt Dip (page 198) • ¼ cup (60 mL) Rhubarb, Apples and Berries (page 93) • ½ cup (125 mL) full-fat (3.5% M.F.) milk	• 1 Nutty Waffle (page 189) • ¼ cup (60 mL) Apricots, Pears and Tofu (page 109) • ½ cup (125 mL) full-fat (3.5% M.F.) milk	• 2 Multigrain Pancakes (page 190) spread with Figgy Pears (page 88) • ½ cup (125 mL) full-fat (3.5% M.F.) milk
Snack	• ½ cup (125 mL) Avocado Banana Yogurt (page 168) • ½ cup (125 mL) apple juice, diluted with water	• 1 Carrot and Date Muffin (page 206) • ½ cup (125 mL) apple juice, diluted with water	• ¼ cup (60 mL) Melon Madness (page 90) • Animal-shaped cookies • ½ cup (125 mL) apple juice, diluted with water

MEAL	1	2	3
Lunch	• Cheese sandwich on whole wheat bread • ¼ cup (60 mL) Orange Banana Smoothie (page 187) • ½ cup (125 mL) full-fat (3.5% M.F.) milk	• ½ cup (125 mL) Guacamole for Beginners (page 89) • Pita wedges • Cubed cheese • ½ cup (125 mL) full-fat (3.5% M.F.) milk	• ½ cup (125 mL) Polenta with Apricots (page 181) • Sliced grapes • ½ cup (125 mL) full-fat (3.5% M.F.) milk
Snack	• ½ cup (125 mL) Fruity Cottage Cheese (page 171) • Whole wheat crackers • Water	• ½ cup (125 mL) Over-the-Top Applesauce (page 174) • Animal-shaped cookies • Water	• ½ cup (125 mL) toasted oat cereal, dry • Fruity Frosty Shake (page 186)
Supper	• ½ cup (125 mL) Chicken with Brown Rice and Peas (page 139) • Cooked carrot coins • ¼ cup (60 mL) Blueberry Apricot Crumble (page 203) • ½ cup (125 mL) full-fat (3.5% M.F.) milk	• ½ cup (125 mL) Chicken Jambalaya (page 136) • Cooked chopped broccoli • ½ cup (125 mL) full-fat (3.5% M.F.) milk	• ¼ cup (60 mL) cooked cubed chicken • ½ cup (125 mL) Broccoli and Cauliflower Melt (page 194) • Sliced ripe pears • ½ cup (125 mL) full-fat (3.5% M.F.) milk
Snack	• ½ banana • ½ cup (125 mL) full-fat (3.5% M.F.) milk	• ½ cup (125 mL) toasted oat cereal, dry • ½ cup (125 mL) full-fat (3.5% M.F.) milk	• 1 Pumpkin Cookie (page 208) • ½ cup (125 mL) full-fat (3.5% M.F.) milk

For a simple, nutritious treat, blend ripe seasonal fruit with ice and milk.

VARIATIONS

Substitute soy or rice beverage for the milk.

Substitute 1 cup (250 mL) frozen fruit purée for the pear and berries and omit the ice.

Fruity Frosty Shake

1 cup	full-fat (3.5% M.F.) milk	250 mL
1/2 cup	crushed ice	125 mL
1/2 cup	chopped peeled pear	125 mL
1/4 cup	frozen berries	60 mL

1. In blender, on high speed, purée milk, ice, pear and berries until smooth and slushy.

Nutritional Information (Per Serving)

Calories	111 Kcal
Total Carbohydrates	15 g
Fiber	2 g
Fat	4 g
Protein	4 g
Iron	0 mg

This is a family favorite and great for a nutritious snack in a hurry!

VARIATION

Substitute chocolate cow's milk for the soy beverage.

Nutty Choco' Monkey

1	banana	1
1 cup	chocolate-flavored soy beverage	250 mL
1/2 cup	crushed ice	125 mL
1/4 cup	smooth peanut butter	60 mL

1. In blender, on high speed, purée banana, soy beverage, ice and peanut butter until smooth.

Nutritional Information (Per Serving)

Calories	350 Kcal
Total Carbohydrates	33 g
Fiber	3 g
Fat	21 g
Protein	3 g
Iron	1 mg

Orange Banana Smoothie

1	banana	1
1 cup	sliced peeled orange (about 1)	250 mL

1. In blender, combine banana and orange and purée on high speed until smooth.

Nutritional Information (Per ¼-cup/60 mL Serving)

Calories . . . . 101 Kcal
Total Carbohydrates . . . . 26 g
Fiber . . . . 3 g
Fat . . . . 0 g
Protein . . . . 1 g
Iron . . . . 0 mg

MAKES ABOUT 2 CUPS (500 ML)

Smoothies are an excellent way to pack extra vitamins and nutrients into your child's day.

TIP

Use whole oranges in place of juice whenever possible. Make sure to remove peel, pith and seeds, which are bitter.

Simple Fruit Sorbet

½ cup	frozen peach purée	125 mL
½ cup	unsweetened apple juice	125 mL

1. In blender, on high speed, purée peach purée and juice until smooth. Serve immediately.

Nutritional Information (Per ½ Serving)

Calories . . . . 131 Kcal
Total Carbohydrates . . . . 33 g
Fiber . . . . 3 g
Fat . . . . 0 g
Protein . . . . 1 g
Iron . . . . 1 mg

MAKES 1 SERVING

Is your freezer still full of containers of delicious fruit purées? Now that your little one is getting older, here is a quick treat idea.

VARIATION

Substitute any fruit purée for the peach purée and any flavor juice for the apple juice.

**MAKES ABOUT
1 CUP (250 ML)**

This recipe can be mixed with formula or with any fruit or vegetable purée to increase fiber intake. Try it in Blueberry Apricot Crumble (page 203) or Blue Nectarine Yogurt (page 201).

TIP

This recipe is suitable for babies nine months and older if the almonds are omitted.

Mixed Grains

Preheat oven to 350°F (180°C)
Rimmed baking sheet

1 cup	old-fashioned rolled oats	250 mL
1/4 cup	bran cereal	60 mL
1/4 cup	unblanched almonds (optional)	60 mL
2 tbsp	wheat germ	30 mL

1. Spread oats, bran cereal, almonds (if using) and wheat germ on baking sheet. Bake in preheated oven until fragrant and lightly toasted, about 7 minutes. Let cool.

2. Transfer toasted grains to blender and purée on high speed until smooth.

3. *Make ahead:* Store in an airtight container in a cool place for up to 1 month.

Nutritional Information **(Per 1/4-cup/60 mL Serving)**	
Calories	158 Kcal
Total Carbohydrates	22 g
Fiber	6 g
Fat	6 g
Protein	6 g
Iron	2 mg

Nutty Waffles

Preheated waffle iron, greased

3	eggs	3
1½ cups	full-fat (3.5% M.F.) milk	375 mL
¼ cup	butter, melted	60 mL
1½ cups	all-purpose flour	375 mL
½ cup	ground toasted pecans or walnuts	125 mL
1 tbsp	baking powder	15 mL
1 tbsp	granulated sugar	15 mL
½ tsp	salt	2 mL

1. In blender, on high speed, purée eggs, milk and butter until smooth. Sprinkle with flour, pecans, baking powder, sugar and salt. Pulse on low speed just until combined (mixture will be lumpy). Do not overmix or waffles will be tough.

2. Spoon ½ cup (125 mL) batter into hot waffle iron, spreading with spatula. Close lid and cook for 5 to 7 minutes, until golden-brown and no longer steaming. Remove to a plate and keep warm. Repeat with remaining batter.

3. *Make ahead:* Store waffles in an airtight container, layered between waxed paper or parchment paper, in the refrigerator for up to 1 day or in the freezer for up to 3 months. To serve, toast frozen waffles in toaster until warmed through.

Nutritional Information (Per Waffle)	
Calories	160 Kcal
Total Carbohydrates	16 g
Fiber	1 g
Fat	9 g
Protein	4 g
Iron	1 mg

MAKES 12 WAFFLES

If you don't have a waffle iron, this batter will work for pancakes too. Top with slices of banana and berries for a treat.

TIP

Toast nuts in a dry skillet over medium-high heat until fragrant, about 3 minutes, to intensify their flavor. Watch carefully — if they scorch, they will be bitter.

Mix up the dry ingredients ahead of time, and your very own nutritious pancake mix will be ready when you are! Store in an airtight container for up to 1 month.

TIP

Add extra nutrients to maple syrup by mixing ¼ cup (60 mL) of your child's favorite fruit purée with ¼ cup (60 mL) maple syrup.

Multigrain Pancakes

3	eggs	3
1½ cups	full-fat (3.5% M.F.) milk	375 mL
¼ cup	butter, melted	60 mL
¼ cup	liquid honey	60 mL
1 cup	whole wheat flour	250 mL
½ cup	all-purpose flour	125 mL
½ cup	old-fashioned rolled oats	125 mL
¼ cup	cornmeal	60 mL
¼ cup	packed brown sugar	60 mL
2 tsp	baking powder	10 mL
1 tsp	salt	5 mL
½ tsp	baking soda	2 mL
½ tsp	ground cinnamon	2 mL
2 tsp	butter (approx.)	10 mL

1. In blender, on high speed, purée eggs, milk, melted butter and honey until smooth. Sprinkle in whole wheat and all-purpose flours, oats, cornmeal, brown sugar, baking powder, salt, baking soda and cinnamon. Pulse on low speed just until combined (mixture will be lumpy). Do not overmix or pancakes will be tough.

2. In a skillet, melt some of the 2 tsp (10 mL) butter over medium heat. Pour in ¼ cup (60 mL) batter for each pancake, leaving room for spreading. Cook until tops of pancakes are speckled with bubbles; turn and cook until undersides are golden, about 1 minute. Remove to a plate and keep warm. Repeat with remaining batter, adding more butter to the skillet as necessary.

3. *Make ahead:* Store pancakes in an airtight container, layered between waxed paper or parchment paper, in the refrigerator for up to 1 day or in the freezer for up to 3 months. To serve, toast frozen pancakes in toaster until warmed through.

Nutritional Information (Per Pancake)	
Calories	138 Kcal
Total Carbohydrates	20 g
Fiber	1 g
Fat	5 g
Protein	4 g
Iron	1 mg

**MAKES 8
CORNCAKES**

*These make great
dippers for soup and
chili — or fill with jam
for a tasty sandwich.*

VARIATIONS

Add 1 cup (250 mL)
corn kernels to batter.

To make small,
handheld snacks,
use 1 tbsp (15 mL)
of the batter to make
each cake.

MAKE AHEAD

Store corncakes in
an airtight container,
layered between waxed
paper or parchment
paper, in the refrigerator
for up to 1 day or in
the freezer for up to
3 months. To serve,
place in a single layer
on a baking sheet
lined with parchment
paper in a 200°F
(100°C) oven until
warmed through,
about 15 minutes.

Buttermilk Corncakes

1	egg yolk	1
3/4 cup	buttermilk	175 mL
1 tbsp	butter, melted	15 mL
1/2 cup	cornmeal	125 mL
1/4 cup	all-purpose flour	60 mL
1 tsp	granulated sugar	5 mL
1/2 tsp	baking soda	2 mL
1/4 tsp	salt	1 mL
2 tsp	vegetable oil (approx.)	10 mL

1. In blender, on high speed, purée egg yolk, buttermilk and butter until smooth. Sprinkle in cornmeal, flour, sugar, baking soda and salt. Pulse on low speed just until combined (mixture will be slightly lumpy).

2. In a skillet, heat 1 tsp (5 mL) of the oil over medium heat. Pour in 1/4 cup (60 mL) batter for each corncake, leaving room for spreading. Cook, turning once, until both sides are golden, about 3 minutes per side. Remove to a plate and keep warm. Repeat with remaining batter, adding oil to the skillet as necessary.

Nutritional Information (Per Corncake)	
Calories	44 Kcal
Total Carbohydrates	6 g
Fiber	0 g
Fat	2 g
Protein	1 g
Iron	trace

Breakfast Toast Strips

MAKES 1 SERVING

These handheld strips are an excellent way to start the day. You can also pack them up for a snack on the go!

1	egg	1
2 tbsp	full-fat (3.5% M.F.) milk	30 mL
½ tsp	vanilla	2 mL
½ tsp	grated orange zest	2 mL
¼ tsp	ground cinnamon	1 mL
2 tsp	butter	10 mL
1	slice whole wheat bread, cut into 1-inch (2.5 cm) strips	1
	Fruity Yogurt Dip (see page 198)	

1. In blender, on high speed, purée egg, milk, vanilla, orange zest and cinnamon until smooth. Transfer to a shallow bowl or pie plate.

2. In a skillet, melt butter over medium heat. Dip bread strips in egg mixture, turning until well coated. Arrange in a single layer in skillet. Cook, turning once, until both sides are golden, about 3 minutes per side. Serve warm with Fruity Yogurt Dip.

Nutritional Information (Per Serving)

Calories . . . . 199 Kcal
Total Carbohydrates . . . . 17 g
Fiber . . . . 2 g
Fat . . . . 11 g
Protein . . . . 9 g
Iron . . . . 2 mg

*Get in the habit of
sprinkling wheat germ
over all your veggies
to sneak in some
extra fiber.*

TIP

Toasting nuts, seeds
and grains brings out
their flavor. Toast them
on a rimmed baking
sheet in a 350°F (180°C)
oven until fragrant and
lightly golden, about
5 minutes. Let cool
before using.

Broccoli and Cauliflower Melt

1 cup	broccoli florets and peeled stems	250 mL
1 cup	cauliflower florets	250 mL
1 cup	full-fat (3.5% M.F.) milk	250 mL
2 tbsp	toasted old-fashioned rolled oats	30 mL
1 tbsp	wheat germ	15 mL
½ cup	shredded Cheddar cheese	125 mL

1. In a medium saucepan, over medium-high heat, combine broccoli, cauliflower, milk, oats and wheat germ; bring to a boil. Cover, reduce heat and simmer until vegetables are very tender, about 20 minutes. Stir in cheese. Let cool.

2. Transfer to blender and purée on high speed until smooth.

**Nutritional Information
(Per ¼-cup/60 mL Serving)**

Calories . . . . 61 Kcal
Total Carbohydrates . . . . 4 g
Fiber . . . . 1 g
Fat . . . . 4 g
Protein . . . . 4 g
Iron . . . . 0 mg

Ham with White Beans and Cabbage

2 tsp	olive oil	10 mL
½ cup	sliced onion	125 mL
½ cup	diced cooked ham (about 4 oz/125 g)	125 mL
2 cups	water or homemade chicken stock (see page 62)	500 mL
½ cup	dried white beans, soaked and drained (see tips, at right)	125 mL
1 cup	chopped green cabbage	250 mL

1. In a medium saucepan, heat oil over medium-high heat. Add onion and cook, stirring, until tender, about 5 minutes. Add ham and cook, stirring, until lightly browned, about 3 minutes. Stir in water, scraping any brown bits from bottom of pan. Add beans; cover, reduce heat and simmer for 30 minutes. Stir in cabbage and simmer until beans and cabbage are tender, about 30 minutes. Let cool.

2. Transfer to blender and purée on high speed to desired consistency.

Nutritional Information
(Per ½-cup/125 mL Serving)

Calories . . . . 173 Kcal
Total Carbohydrates . . . . 20 g
Fiber . . . . 5 g
Fat . . . . 2 g
Protein . . . . 15 g
Iron . . . . 3 mg

MAKES ABOUT 2 CUPS (500 ML)

Most varieties of dried beans are excellent sources of potassium and folic acid, and they give a smooth, creamy consistency to purées.

TIPS

Soaking beans and legumes overnight decreases cooking time, preserves nutrients and reduces the flatulence they can cause.

Quick soak method: In a saucepan, combine 3 parts water with 1 part dried beans; bring to a boil over medium heat. Remove from heat and let stand, covered, for 1 to 2 hours. Drain. Cook according to recipe.

Add homemade vegetable stock or more chicken stock to make a great soup for the whole family.

*Try this sauce over
pastini or stirred into
any meat purée to boost
nutritional value and
flavor.*

Veggie Cream Sauce

1 tbsp	olive oil	15 mL
1 cup	diced peeled carrots (about 2)	250 mL
1/2 cup	diced peeled broccoli stems	125 mL
1/4 cup	diced onion	60 mL
1	clove garlic, minced	1
2 tbsp	cubed softened cream cheese	30 mL
1 cup	water or homemade chicken stock (see page 62)	250 mL

1. In a skillet, heat oil over medium-high heat. Stir in carrots, broccoli, onion and garlic; cook, stirring often, until carrots are tender, about 5 minutes. Whisk in cream cheese and water; bring just to a boil. Reduce heat and simmer, uncovered, until vegetables are very tender, about 10 minutes. Let cool.

2. Transfer to blender and purée on high speed until very smooth.

**Nutritional Information
(Per 1/4-cup/60 mL Serving)**

Calories . . . . 33 Kcal
Total Carbohydrates . . . . 4 g
Fiber . . . . 1 g
Fat . . . . 2 g
Protein . . . . 1 g
Iron . . . . 0 mg

Veggie Red Sauce

1 tbsp	olive oil	15 mL
1	clove garlic, minced	1
1 cup	chopped peeled carrots (about 2)	250 mL
½ cup	chopped peeled broccoli stems	125 mL
¼ cup	chopped onion	60 mL
1 cup	canned diced tomatoes, with juice	250 mL

1. In a skillet, heat oil over medium-high heat. Add garlic, carrots, broccoli stems and onion and stir to combine. Cook, stirring, until carrots are tender, about 7 minutes. Add tomatoes with juice, reduce heat and simmer until vegetables are very tender, about 15 minutes. Let cool.

2. Transfer to blender and purée on high speed until very smooth.

MAKES 2 CUPS (500 ML)

Sometimes we have to be a bit sneaky when our toddlers are going through a "non-veggie" stage... what they don't know can be good for them!

TIP

Use this sauce in any recipe that calls for prepared pasta sauce.

**Nutritional Information
(Per ¼-cup/60 mL Serving)**

Calories	33 Kcal
Total Carbohydrates	4 g
Fiber	1 g
Fat	2 g
Protein	1 g
Iron	0 mg

12

*There will come a point
when the only way to
get your child to eat is
to serve a dip alongside.
Here are some quick,
easy, nutritious options.*

VARIATION

Substitute 1 cup
(250 mL) of any fruit
purée you have stored
in your freezer for the
options given here.
Thaw before blending.

Fruity Yogurt and Cream Cheese Dips

Yogurt Base

| ½ cup | full-fat (3.5% M.F.) plain yogurt | 125 mL |
| 1 tbsp | liquid honey | 15 mL |

1. In blender, on low speed, blend yogurt and honey
until smooth.

2. Blend with any of the fruit combinations that follow.

3. *Make ahead:* Store in an airtight container in the
refrigerator for up to 3 days.

Nutritional Information (Per ½ Recipe)			
Calories	70 Kcal	Fat	2 g
Total Carbohydrates	11 g	Protein	2 g
Fiber	0 g	Iron	0 mg

Cream Cheese Base

| 4 oz | spreadable cream cheese (½ package) | 125 g |
| ¼ cup | full-fat (3.5% M.F.) milk | 60 mL |

1. In blender, on low speed, blend cream cheese and
milk until smooth.

2. Blend with any of the fruit combinations that follow.

3. *Make ahead:* Store in an airtight container in the
refrigerator for up to 3 days.

Nutritional Information (Per ½ Recipe)			
Calories	217 Kcal	Fat	21 g
Total Carbohydrates	3 g	Protein	5 g
Fiber	0 g	Iron	1 mg

Banana and Mango

| 1 | small banana, chopped | 1 |
| 1/2 cup | chopped peeled mango | 125 mL |

Nutritional Information (Per 1/2 Recipe)		
Calories	81 Kcal	Fat	0 g
Total Carbohydrates	21 g	Protein	1 g
Fiber	2 g	Iron	0 mg

Apple and Apricot

1/2 cup	chopped peeled apple	125 mL
1/2 cup	chopped peeled apricots	125 mL
1/4 tsp	ground cinnamon	1 mL

Nutritional Information (Per 1/2 Recipe)		
Calories	36 Kcal	Fat	0 g
Total Carbohydrates	9 g	Protein	1 g
Fiber	2 g	Iron	0 mg

Peach and Orange

| 1/2 cup | chopped peeled peach | 125 mL |
| 1/2 cup | orange segments, white pith removed | 125 mL |

Nutritional Information (Per 1/2 Recipe)		
Calories	39 Kcal	Fat	0 g
Total Carbohydrates	10 g	Protein	1 g
Fiber	2 g	Iron	0 mg

Continued on next page

199

Tangerine and Kiwi

| ½ cup | tangerine segments | 125 mL |
| ½ cup | chopped peeled kiwi | 125 mL |

Nutritional Information (Per ½ Recipe)			
Calories	48 Kcal	Fat	0 g
Total Carbohydrates	12 g	Protein	1 g
Fiber	3 g	Iron	0 mg

Strawberry and Lemon

1 cup	sliced strawberries	250 mL
1 tsp	grated lemon zest	5 mL
2 tsp	freshly squeezed lemon juice	10 mL

Nutritional Information (Per ½ Recipe)			
Calories	27 Kcal	Fat	0 g
Total Carbohydrates	6 g	Protein	1 g
Fiber	2 g	Iron	0 mg

Pear and Ginger

| 1 cup | chopped peeled pear | 250 mL |
| ½ tsp | ground ginger | 2 mL |

Nutritional Information (Per ½ Recipe)			
Calories	51 Kcal	Fat	0 g
Total Carbohydrates	13 g	Protein	0 g
Fiber	2 g	Iron	0 mg

Blue Nectarine Yogurt

1 cup	sliced nectarines (about 2)	250 mL
¼ cup	fresh or thawed frozen blueberries	60 mL
1 cup	plain yogurt	250 mL
1 cup	Mixed Grains (see page 188)	250 mL

1. Place nectarines and blueberries in blender and purée on high speed until smooth.

2. Transfer to a medium bowl and stir in yogurt.

3. For each serving, mix ¼ cup (60 mL) yogurt mixture with 2 tbsp (30 mL) Mixed Grains. Let sit for 5 minutes before serving.

Nutritional Information (Per ¼-cup/60 mL Serving)	
Calories	136 Kcal
Total Carbohydrates	18 g
Fiber	4 g
Fat	5 g
Protein	5 g
Iron	0 mg

MAKES ABOUT 2 CUPS (500 ML)

Cereals based on oats provide long-lasting energy throughout the day. Mix them with your child's favorite fruit, yogurt or cottage cheese to get them through action-packed days.

TIP

Add milk to each serving as desired for a thinner consistency.

12

**MAKES ABOUT
2 CUPS (500 ML)**

*Raspberries and
blueberries are packed
with nutrients, but are
too strong to offer to
your baby on their own.
Adding a few into pears
is an economical, tasty
solution.*

TIP

This recipe is suitable
for babies six months
and older if the honey
is omitted.

FOR OLDER KIDS

Turn ordinary porridge
into something special
by mixing in some of
this purée, along with
a sprinkle of toasted
almonds.

Very Berry Pears

3 cups	diced peeled pears (about 4)	750 mL
1/2 cup	water (approx.)	125 mL
1/4 cup	raspberries	60 mL
1/4 cup	blueberries	60 mL
1 tbsp	liquid honey (optional)	15 mL

1. In a medium saucepan, over medium-low heat, combine pears, water, raspberries, blueberries and honey (if using). Cover and simmer, stirring occasionally, until pears are very tender, about 30 minutes. Let cool.

2. Transfer to blender and purée on high speed, adding more water if necessary, until smooth.

**Nutritional Information
(Per 1/4-cup/60 mL Serving)**

Calories . . . . 44 Kcal
Total Carbohydrates . . . . 11 g
Fiber . . . . 2 g
Fat . . . . 0 g
Protein . . . . 0 g
Iron . . . . 0 mg

Blueberry Apricot Crumble

1 ½ cups	sliced pitted apricots (4 to 5)	375 mL
½ cup	frozen wild blueberries, thawed	125 mL
¼ cup	orange juice	60 mL
½ cup	Mixed Grains (see page 88)	125 mL

1. Place apricots, blueberries and orange juice in blender and purée on high speed until smooth.

2. Sprinkle with Mixed Grains. For softer grains, let sit for 5 minutes before serving.

Nutritional Information (Per ¼-cup/60 mL Serving)	
Calories	59 Kcal
Total Carbohydrates	9 g
Fiber	2 g
Fat	2 g
Protein	2 g
Iron	0 mg

MAKES ABOUT 2 CUPS (500 ML)

These two fruits are nutritional dynamos and provide a wonderful meal when combined with energy-boosting grains.

TIPS

When apricots are not in season, substitute dried apricots, which have a higher concentration of nutrients. Soak them in enough boiling water just to cover them for 30 minutes before using.

Top with a dollop of plain yogurt.

Squashed Apples make these fiber-filled muffins moist and delicious.

Squashed Apple and Bran Mini Muffins

1	egg	1
1 cup	Squashed Apples (see page 80)	250 mL
2/3 cup	buttermilk	150 mL
1/3 cup	lightly packed brown sugar	75 mL
1/4 cup	fancy molasses	60 mL
1/4 cup	vegetable oil	60 mL
1 tsp	vanilla	5 mL
1 cup	natural wheat bran	250 mL
1 cup	whole wheat flour	250 mL
1 cup	unbleached all-purpose flour	250 mL
1 tsp	baking soda	5 mL
1/2 tsp	salt	2 mL
1 cup	raisins (optional)	250 mL

1. Line 24 mini muffin cups with paper liners or grease; set aside. Preheat oven to 375°F (190°C).

2. In a medium bowl, whisk together egg, Squashed Apples, buttermilk, brown sugar, molasses, oil and vanilla until well blended. Stir in bran and let soften for about 5 minutes.

3. In a large bowl, whisk together whole wheat flour, all-purpose flour, baking soda and salt. Pour apple mixture and raisins (if using) over dry ingredients and stir until just combined.

4. Spoon into prepared muffin cups, filling to top. Bake in preheated oven until tops are golden and firm to touch, about 12 minutes. Let cool in pans on rack.

Nutritional Information
Serving 2 mini muffins

Calories	200 Kcal
Total Carbohydrates	33 g
Fiber	4 g
Fat	6 g
Protein	5 g
Iron	2.2 mg

Using a fruit purée in muffins can lower the amount of sugar and fat needed for baking, and they still taste great.

Carrot and Date Muffins

1 cup	whole wheat flour	250 mL
¾ cup	unbleached all-purpose flour	175 mL
¼ cup	brown sugar	60 mL
1½ tsp	baking powder	7 mL
1 tsp	cinnamon	5 mL
½ tsp	baking soda	2 mL
½ tsp	salt	2 mL
2	eggs	2
1 cup	Carrot and Date purée (see page 65)	250 mL
¼ cup	vegetable oil	60 mL
1 tsp	vanilla	5 mL

1. Line 12 muffin cups with paper liners or grease; set aside. Preheat oven to 375°F (190°C).

2. In a large bowl, whisk together flours, brown sugar, baking powder, cinnamon, baking soda and salt.

3. In a medium bowl, whisk together eggs, carrot and date purée, oil and vanilla. Stir into dry ingredients just until moistened. (Over-mixing will make muffins tough.) Spoon into prepared cups.

4. Bake in center of preheated oven until tops are golden and firm to touch, about 20 minutes. Let cool on rack.

**Nutritional Information
Serving 1 muffin**

Calories . . . . .160 Kcal
Total Carbohydrates . . . . .24 g
Fiber . . . . .2 g
Fat. . . . . .6 g
Protein . . . . .4 g
Iron. . . . . .1 mg

Instant Banana Berry "Ice Cream"

1	frozen banana	1
1 cup	frozen berries	250 mL

1. Place bananas and berries in blender. Purée on high speed until smooth and serve immediately. Freeze any unused portions.

**Nutritional Information
(Per ¼-cup/60 mL Serving)**

Calories . . . . .22 Kcal
Total Carbohydrates . . . . .5 g
Fiber . . . . .1 g
Fat . . . . .0 g
Protein . . . . 0.3 g
Iron . . . . 0 mg

**MAKES ABOUT
2 CUPS (500 ML)**

*Easiest ice cream ever!!!
You won't be just
making this for baby…*

Offer these guilt-free cookies at your next playdate, and you will be the hit of your parents group!

Pumpkin Cookies

1 cup	Pumpkin purée (see page 36)	250 mL
1/2 cup	brown sugar	125 mL
1/4 cup	vegetable oil	60 mL
1	egg	1
1 tbsp	vanilla	15 mL
1 1/2 cups	large flake rolled oats	375 mL
1 cup	whole wheat flour	250 mL
1 tsp	cinnamon	5 mL
1/2 tsp	baking powder	2 mL
1/2 tsp	baking soda	2 mL
1/4 tsp	salt	1 mL

1. Preheat oven to 350°F (180°C). Line rimmed baking sheets with parchment paper; set aside.

2. In a large bowl, whisk together pumpkin purée, brown sugar, oil, egg and vanilla.

3. In a separate bowl, whisk together oats, flour, cinnamon, baking powder, baking soda and salt. Pour over pumpkin mixture and stir well to combine.

4. Using a spoon, scoop out dough by the rounded tablespoon (15 mL) and shape into a ball. Place 2 inches (5 cm) apart on prepared baking sheet; flatten slightly with a fork. Bake in oven until golden, about 10 minutes.

5. Let cool one minute before transferring to rack to cool completely. Repeat with remaining dough.

Nutritional Information Serving 1 cookie	
Calories	82 Kcal
Total Carbohydrates	12 g
Fiber	1 g
Fat	3 g
Protein	2 g
Iron	0.7 mg

Library and Archives Canada Cataloguing in Publication

Young, Nicole
    Blender baby food : over 175 recipes for healthy homemade meals /
Nicole Young ; Nadine Day, nutritional advisor. — 2nd ed.

Includes index.
ISBN 978-0-7788-0262-4

    1. Cooking (Baby foods). 2. Baby foods. 3. Blenders (Cooking).
4. Infants—Nutrition. I. Title.

TX740.Y68124 2011   641.5'6222   C2010-907369-X

Index